Pedigree Dogs

in Needle Felt

Dedication

This book is dedicated to Megan.
My first little needle-felted dog was born
because of you.

Pedigree Dogs
in Needle Felt

GAI BUTTON

Search Press

First published in 2015

Search Press Limited
Wellwood, North Farm Road,
Tunbridge Wells, Kent TN2 3DR

Text copyright © Gai Button, 2015
Photographs by Paul Bricknell at Search Press Studios
Photographs and design copyright © Search Press Ltd 2015

ISBN: 978-1-78221-034-4

The Publishers and author can accept no responsibility for
any consequences arising from the information, advice or
instructions given in this publication.

Readers are permitted to reproduce any of the items in this
book for their personal use, or for the purpose of selling for
charity, free of charge and without the prior permission of the
Publishers. Any use of the items for commercial purposes is not
permitted without the prior permission of the Publishers.

Suppliers

If you have difficulty in obtaining any of the materials and
equipment mentioned in this book, then please visit the
Search Press website for details of suppliers:
www.searchpress.com

You are invited to visit the author's website:
www.gaibutton.co.uk

Printed in China

Acknowledgements

I would like to thank:
Kite, our standard poodle for
being my constant companion
throughout writing this book,
along with darling BlueBell and
Lulu – now over the rainbow –
for being my first inspiration.

All of my family and friends, for
giving much-needed support
while playing second fiddle to
needles and wool.

Chris, for reassuring me that making the same dog a
hundred times is not time wasted but 'development'.
Andrea for accepting that where I go little heads on
sticks will always follow!
Sara-Jane, for helping me feel positive
when negative thoughts crept in.
Mum, for giving me encouragement with my
crafts from early childhood to now.
Thanks too to special friends Cathy, for sharing
expert knowledge of real dogs, and Lynne, for
making the cute little neckerchief.
Thank you to lovely Katherine Jewitt, for
starting the ball rolling by first finding space
for me in a craft publication.

Special thanks go to my suppliers for all the help,
advice and quality tools and fibre used for
making the little dogs in the book.
World of Wool, for my ideal core wool; without you I
may never have found my now favourite Southdown.
Wingham Wool Work, for supplying top-coat wool
and needles, and a special thank you for sourcing the
reverse felting needles that I love.
Coats Crafts UK, for the fabulous felting yarn.
Clover Mfg. Co. Ltd Japan, for the perfect little tool.

Last but not least, the people who made this book
possible: All the friendly Search Press team, especially
Roz, for believing in me enough to commission
this book and Edd, for his incredible editing skills,
supplied in a kind and reassuring manner. Paul, for
photographing such miniscule amounts of wool and
keeping a sense of humour throughout!

Thank you all so very much.

Contents

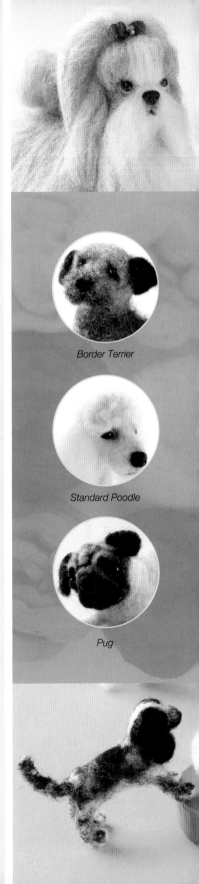

Introduction

I discovered needle felting at a local craft exhibition when a demonstrator gave me a needle to punch into some bright red wool. I was fascinated how the soft fibres could be worked into shape with a single barbed needle. Enthralled, I bought felting wool and needles to continue my new hobby at home.

Keen to improve my needle felting skills, I experimented and began making little dogs. I wanted them to look as realistic as possible. Practice makes perfect and I became proficient at needling even the tiniest detail. I found that making my own polymer clay sculpted eyes and noses gave me the flexibility to make any size, shape or colour that I chose and they would fit the dogs perfectly. Eyelashes softened tiny eyes and claws could be added to a chubby little puppy's paws. There was always something new to learn and with so many breeds of dog, lack of variety was not a problem.

Hidden away in a cupboard I have a box of misshapes, little unfinished woolly dogs that are waiting to be transformed by a felting needle. The great thing about this craft is that nothing is ever wasted – if you are not happy with your labrador because it looks more like a beagle, turn it into one, or brush out the wool and start again! It is not a mistake if you have learned something, and sometimes happy accidents happen. Needle felting is not an exact science and you will develop your own way of working that suits you. All good artists eventually find their own style.

Each of the projects in this book is designed to increase your repertoire of skills in a user-friendly way. Step-by-step instructions, diagrams and pictures will lead you through the process of making each dog. You will be shown techniques to make the tiny dogs look convincingly life-like and, as your confidence grows, you will be able to take elements from the different dog projects and, in a mix-and-match fashion, combine them to needle felt the breed, pose and colour pedigree pooch of your choice.

Needle felting is a wonderful craft that is not too difficult or expensive, and everything you need to complete a project can be popped in a small bag and carried anywhere. Instead of doodling a poodle, with a little help from this book you could try needle felting one.

Enjoy!

Materials and tools

Wool

There are many different types of wool and while most will needle felt, some are definitely better to use than others. Suppliers can often give a good description of colour, feel and length of the fibre, but be careful when reading the description, as 'suitable for hand felting' could refer to the method of using soap and water (wet felting) rather than the needle-and-pad method used in this book.

Wool may be chosen for a variety of reasons and to some extent it is a personal preference but availability, price, look, feel and the ease and speed with which the wool felts up are all to be taken into consideration. For the dogs in this book, I suggest you use carded wool tops because the uniform lengths make it possible to measure out small portions of wool. This is helpful when working out how wool much you will need for a project or for carding together the correct colour mix.

To help you decide which wool to buy you must first understand the two basic elements of your needle-felted dog's construction: the core and the top coat.

Core wool

The inner part of your dog sculpture is called the 'core'. This is covered by the outer top coat. Although unseen, this first layer plays an important role in the basic structure of your dog. Wool that needle felts quickly and easily is the best type to use for the core. It also needs to give a uniform finish. Lumps and bumps on these small sculptures can be a problem, so fleece needs to be carded. Your fingers will help to mould and smooth your dog into shape so choose wool that holds firm but is still spongy and pliable rather than stiff and dense. Lustrous wool that slips when you wind it around the wires is not ideal for the core. Instead, look for wool with a good crimp and choose short fibres that make it easier to tear apart.

I picked, prodded, and poked my way through a massive amount of natural wool to find my three favourites. They are all carded wool tops: Southdown, whitefaced woodland and Dorset horn. Much to my amazement, they are wools that I had never knowingly used before. I love the way the needle catches on the short crimped fibres and speedily felts them together. I also like the feel of the felted wool after the needle has done its work – nice and even but just a little rough to the touch, perfect for the top-coat fibres to cling to.

If the core wool is the same colour and texture as the dog you are making, then you can use the same wool all the way through. This is also the better option if a dog is very small and it is not practical to do otherwise.

Top coat wool

The outer part of your dog is referred to as the 'top coat.' This challenging but fun final layer is chosen to replicate the dog's fur. For the top coat, having the correct mix of colour and texture is far more important than ease of needling. Be brave and experiment with different fibres. As long as it looks right and will attach to the core with a barbed needle, any wool will work.

There is a vast array of fibres out there that, with a bit of patience, can be transformed into exquisite life-like fur. If it is too difficult to needle in, try carding with some wool of a similar colour. Tapestry wool is useful for the times when you need only a tiny amount of top coat wool. Pull it apart with your fingers or use the carders to rough it up. Yarn can also be utilised to good effect, as you will see from thick felting wool yarn used in the shih tzu project on pages 58–71. Even the family pet might be happy to oblige you with a combing or two!

Yarn wool and tapestry wool, used for the top coat.

Opposite
Carded wool tops in a various colours.

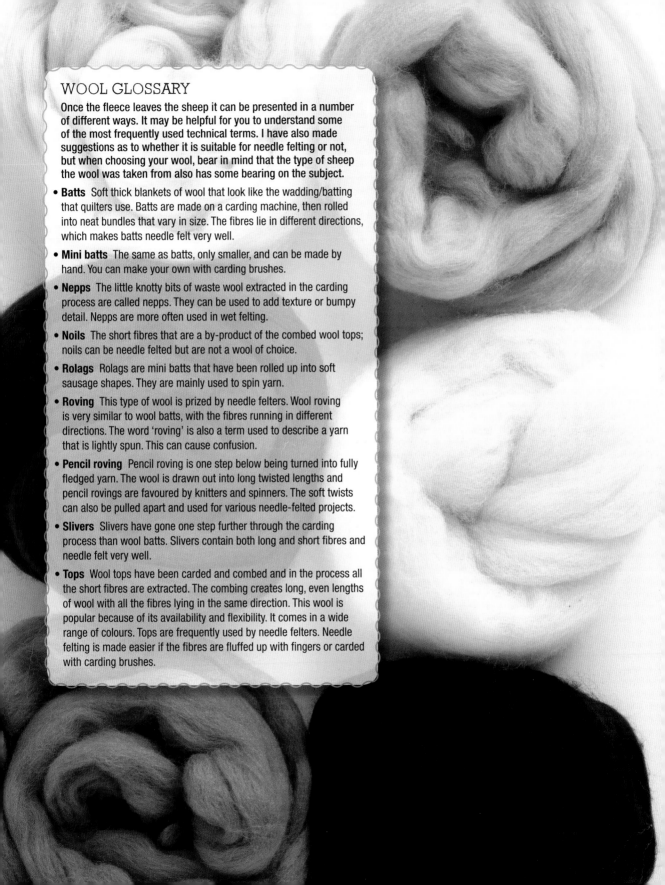

WOOL GLOSSARY

Once the fleece leaves the sheep it can be presented in a number of different ways. It may be helpful for you to understand some of the most frequently used technical terms. I have also made suggestions as to whether it is suitable for needle felting or not, but when choosing your wool, bear in mind that the type of sheep the wool was taken from also has some bearing on the subject.

- **Batts** Soft thick blankets of wool that look like the wadding/batting that quilters use. Batts are made on a carding machine, then rolled into neat bundles that vary in size. The fibres lie in different directions, which makes batts needle felt very well.

- **Mini batts** The same as batts, only smaller, and can be made by hand. You can make your own with carding brushes.

- **Nepps** The little knotty bits of waste wool extracted in the carding process are called nepps. They can be used to add texture or bumpy detail. Nepps are more often used in wet felting.

- **Noils** The short fibres that are a by-product of the combed wool tops; noils can be needle felted but are not a wool of choice.

- **Rolags** Rolags are mini batts that have been rolled up into soft sausage shapes. They are mainly used to spin yarn.

- **Roving** This type of wool is prized by needle felters. Wool roving is very similar to wool batts, with the fibres running in different directions. The word 'roving' is also a term used to describe a yarn that is lightly spun. This can cause confusion.

- **Pencil roving** Pencil roving is one step below being turned into fully fledged yarn. The wool is drawn out into long twisted lengths and pencil rovings are favoured by knitters and spinners. The soft twists can also be pulled apart and used for various needle-felted projects.

- **Slivers** Slivers have gone one step further through the carding process than wool batts. Slivers contain both long and short fibres and needle felt very well.

- **Tops** Wool tops have been carded and combed and in the process all the short fibres are extracted. The combing creates long, even lengths of wool with all the fibres lying in the same direction. This wool is popular because of its availability and flexibility. It comes in a wide range of colours. Tops are frequently used by needle felters. Needle felting is made easier if the fibres are fluffed up with fingers or carded with carding brushes.

Felting needles and pad

A felting needle has a very sharp tip that enables it to plunge through dense fibre. It has a straight round shaft with a barbed working end. These barbs catch up on the scales of the wool and knot them together as the needle is pushed in and out, which forms the matted fibres of the felt.

Felting needles are sold by gauge and shape. The gauge refers to the diameter of the needle, with higher numbers indicating finer needles. Lower gauge needles have larger barbs, which quickly pull the wool fibres into shape. Bigger barbs are not so good at catching tiny amounts of fibre and moving it into place; this is delicate work that requires the small barbs found on the finer-gauged needles. Usually a lower gauge of needle is used to start the work and the higher gauge to finish.

The shape, usually triangle (T) or star (S), refers to the cross-section of the needle. Most of the frequently used felting needles have three working edges which form a triangle; hence the name. Star-shaped needles have a fourth working edge which helps to felt up the wool more quickly.

A felting pad is used as a barrier to prevent the sharp point of the needle sticking into your work surface. You can buy high-density foam pads that are sold especially for the purpose but I find a sponge dish washing pad ideal for small work. I also use upholstery sponge or packing foam.

FELTING NEEDLE GUIDE

- For general needle felting, start with a **standard** needle for the preliminary needling, then change to a **fine** needle until the wool is felted to the desired shape.
- Use a **standard** needle for fusing and implanting pieces.
- For delicate or detailed work, finishing, or if you are using a particularly fine wool, use a **fine** needle.

Needles required for the projects

The three needles – two felting and one reverse felting – that I have chosen for this book will perform all the tasks required to complete the dogs. There is more detail on each type below, but the felting needle guide (see box, below left) will provide all the information you need to get started, and help you decide when and where to use each needle. You may have other preferences – some needle felters favour using only one needle, while others use a number, for example – and if this is the case for you, I encourage you to use whatever needles you feel most comfortable using.

Standard felting needle

Referred to as a 'standard needle' in this book, these are any general-purpose felting needles that work well with different types of wool. Standard needles are sturdier and less likely to break than finer gauges of needle. This is a definite advantage for beginners when needling around the armature wires or implanting parts.

My choice is a 36 gauge triangle (36T). The large barbs of this needle are able to felt deeply, and will shape and move the wool successfully; qualities which make it an ideal needle for starting out the projects.

Fine felting needle

Referred to as 'fine needles' throughout this book, these will penetrate a firmly felted sculpture with ease and allow you to shape small parts that a heavier needle might distort. If the fibre you are using is very fine, a fine needle can be used for every stage; but for coarser fibres, a fine needle will work better once the fibres have been worked into shape by a standard needle. This needle will do a good job at tidying up any stray unruly fibres, making for a nice clean finish. Fine needles will break easily, so be careful.

The extra barbs of a finer needle like a 38 gauge star (38S) means that it felts the fibres quickly, and this is my preferred fine needle. The small barbs are placed nearer to the end of the shaft than in standard felting needles, so use a shallow poking action. A good alternative fine needle is a 40 gauge triangle (40T).

Reverse felting needle

The barbs on the reverse or inverted needle face upwards, so they draw the fibres outwards rather than felting them in. Aside from this, they are used in the same way as a standard felting needle. Referred to throughout the book as 'reverse needles', these can be used for particular effects such as the wiry coat of the border terrier, feathered edges on legs and tails or for puffing up wrinkles on the pug's head. I use a 32 gauge reverse felting needle for some of the projects in this book, and a 40 gauge reverse felting needle, which draws out a little less wool, for others.

Felting needle points. Top to bottom: standard, fine, reverse.

Felting needles in a sponge felting pad. I use paper or felted beads to mark out and organise particular needles to save me having to check the needle size and type when I am working.

Other materials

Carders Also called carding brushes, these have fine wire teeth. Two carders are used together for brushing, disentangling, cleaning and colour mixing wool.

Beads Black glass beads make good eyes.

Embroidery needle These needles, with a large hole and pointed tip, are used for making holes and indentations in the felt or moving and scratching at the wool. They will take several threads at once, which is essential for sewing on eyes.

Beading needle A beading needle will enable you to pull a double thread through a small bead hole.

Chenille sticks Also called pipe cleaners, these make good armatures for your dogs. The soft brush on the pipe cleaner helps to grip the wool, which makes it easier than using smooth wire.

Strong embroidery thread Any colour thread or cord will do as it is glued to the back of the polymer clay eye and will not be seen.

Strong black sewing thread This is used for sewing on bead eyes.

Silk fibre I use silk fibre to make realistic looking claws. Silk will also give a shine to a long-haired dog's coat.

Polymer clay and tile You will need a ceramic tile or other smooth, flat ovenproof surface for moulding and baking the polymer clay, and access to an oven for hardening it. For the projects you will need white for eyes and black for noses. If you are making a batch – of noses, for example – it is a good idea to experiment with browns and skin colours too.

Pins Glass-headed pins make good eye markers and can be easily seen when pinning into wool.

Glue White glue is used for coating silk to make claws for the dogs (see page 110); fast-acting white glue for gluing on noses; and superglue for attaching polymer clay.

Acrylic paints and fine paintbrush I used the following coloured paints for painting the polymer clay eyes: Mars black, raw umber, cadmium yellow.

Gloss varnish Use varnish that is compatible with polymer clay for the handmade eyes.

Claw and mat cleaner tool I use a metal claw for delicate combing of the yarn. Beginners will also find it useful for holding small parts.

Cocktail sticks These are used for winding wool and also stamping colour onto polymer clay eyes.

Drill bit A 2mm (1/16in) drill bit is used to make a hole at the back of the polymer clay eyes.

Fine sandpaper This is used for finishing polymer clay eyes and noses. Alternatively, you could use a nail file.

Masking tape and card These are used to make a sticky board that helps hold polymer clay eyes in place while you prepare them.

Tracing paper If you do not have access to a photocopier, use tracing paper and pencil to make ear templates.

Pen, pliers and wire cutters These are used for marking, bending and cutting chenille sticks.

Skewers Wooden barbecue skewers can be used for winding wool.

Scissors Good quality cuticle scissors work well when trimming the small dogs. Use ordinary scissors for all other cutting.

Sock, gravel and wadding/batting A grey sock, weighted with aquarium gravel, is used as the base for the shih tzu project (see pages 58–71). 1.5cm (1/2in) thick wadding/batting is used for making a pocket to go inside the shih tzu sock.

Ruler A ruler or tape measure is used for measuring lengths of wool yarn.

Concave bead tool A concave bead tool will press out hemispheres of polymer clay that are perfect for handmade eyes.

Techniques

Wool has a mind of its own, but by learning a few techniques it is possible to tame its wild side. The following pages explain how to prepare and measure your wool, and how to get it to lie flat, twist, roll into a ball, or even grab onto a stick. With a bit of patience and careful handling, wool will do what you want it to do, just like a dog!

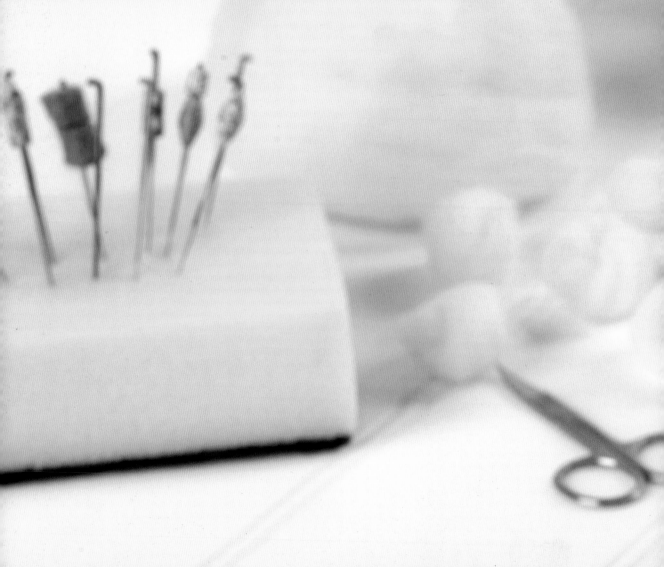

Preparing wool

The techniques on these pages are both part of a single process that lead towards making a correct measure of wool, which is essential to needle felting.

Making a measure: pull and pile

This technique is used to make short, even lengths of wool which are the first stage of making a measure. This method can also be used to create an organised blend of mixed colours that can be implanted to create a long coat.

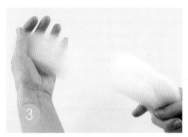

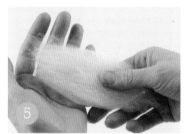

1 Hold the wool firmly in your right hand around 15cm (6in) from the end, then use your left hand to lightly pull it out into a length, as shown.

2 Use your left hand to take hold of the loose fibres at the end and gently draw them away from the length of wool.

3 Holding the separated loose fibres in your hand, repeat three or four times to get a handful of wool. At this point you will have an uneven pile of wool in your hand, with shorter and longer lengths.

4 Hold the handful of wool in one hand and draw the longer lengths from the top, pulling them through and out.

5 Pile them back on the handful and repeat the process until the handful is roughly even, with no long bits sticking out from the top or bottom.

Making a measure: rolling

This technique is used to shape and adjust the even lengths of wool, produced from the pull-and-pile technique, to make one measure.

1 Pinch one end of a handful of wool, pulled and piled as shown on page 16. Use your other hand to gently shape it into a rough cylinder. If you find any lumps or bumps, pull them out and repeat the pull-and-pile technique as necessary to smooth out the length of wool.

2 Pinch both ends and roll the handful into a slightly tighter shape, as shown. Repeat the pull-and-pile technique if you need to shorten the length of the measure.

3 Place the cylinder over the measurement template (see below). Ensure that the ends are within the two lines, and that you can just see the lines around the wool as shown. This gives you one master measure.

Wool measurement template

Please refer to page 21 where you can see a photograph of ready-to-use measures made using this template and the techniques on these pages.

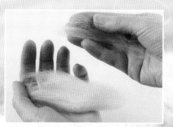

GETTING YOUR MEASURE CORRECT

If there is too much wool, you can simply pull out a small amount – either from the end (see left image), or from the side if you want to remove a particular lump – put it to one side, then pull and pile the remainder. If there is not enough, take a small amount of wool and pile it on (see right image), then pull and pile it until the handful forms a smooth, even cylinder.

Creating a web of wool

Webs of wool can be gossamer-thin and needled in layers to blend and soften colours or thicker to cover flaws in the felt.

1 Pull out a small amount of wool and gently draw it apart from the centre, as shown.

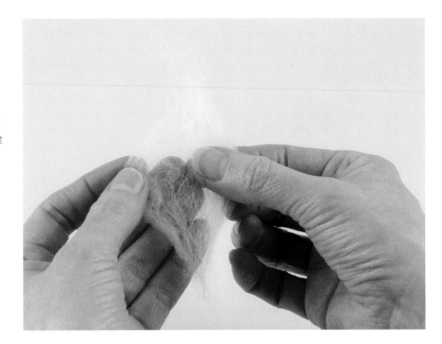

2 Continue to tease it out to create a gossamer-thin 'cobweb' of wool.

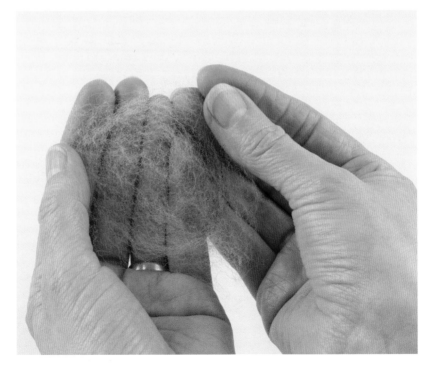

Creating a thread of wool

Manipulating the wool into threads is a helpful technique to use where less fluff and more precision are required.

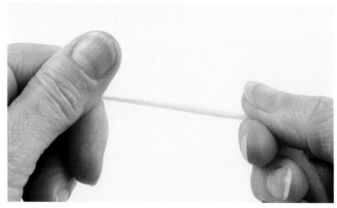

1 Pull out a small amount of wool and gently draw it out into a length.

2 Twist the length between your fingers, starting from the middle and working outwards.

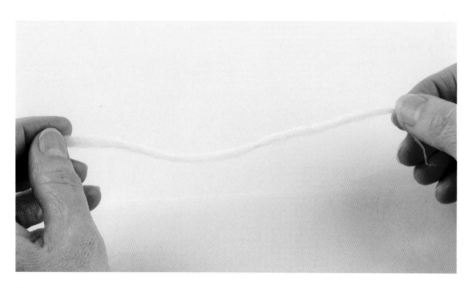

3 Continue twisting to the ends, creating a long, thin and even thread of wool.

Dividing the measures accurately

Accurate measures are important to ensure the finished dogs end up with the correct proportions. Lay the measures side by side on a contrasting coloured surface or cloth and then any slightly bigger or smaller ones will stand out. A textured cloth will help to hold them in place.

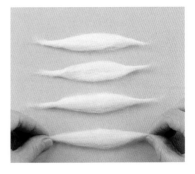

1 To get half measures, make a measure (see pages 16–17) and gently pull it apart, judging it by eye. Roll the pieces, then leave them for a few moments to regain their shape – pulling compresses them.

2 If the two end up at slightly different sizes, gently pull out a little from the larger one. Divide the wool between the two half measures, then repeat the pull-and-pile and roll techniques (see pages 16 and 17) until they are the same size.

3 This process can be repeated for the smaller measures; dividing each half measure into half again for quarter measures, as shown. You can repeat this until you have sixteenths, which are the smallest sizes you will commonly use. Pull and pile at every stage to ensure the pieces keep a good even shape and do not get drawn out.

20

PREPARATION

It is a good idea to prepare lots of wool to save time and keep things consistent. Keep bags of each measure labelled with the type of wool (Southdown, for example) and the measurement size.

To save space and keep each measure together, tie them in loose knots. Note that the wool will be a little compressed when you untie them. Allow it time to expand before use.

The main measures you will use for the dogs in this book, shown at actual size.

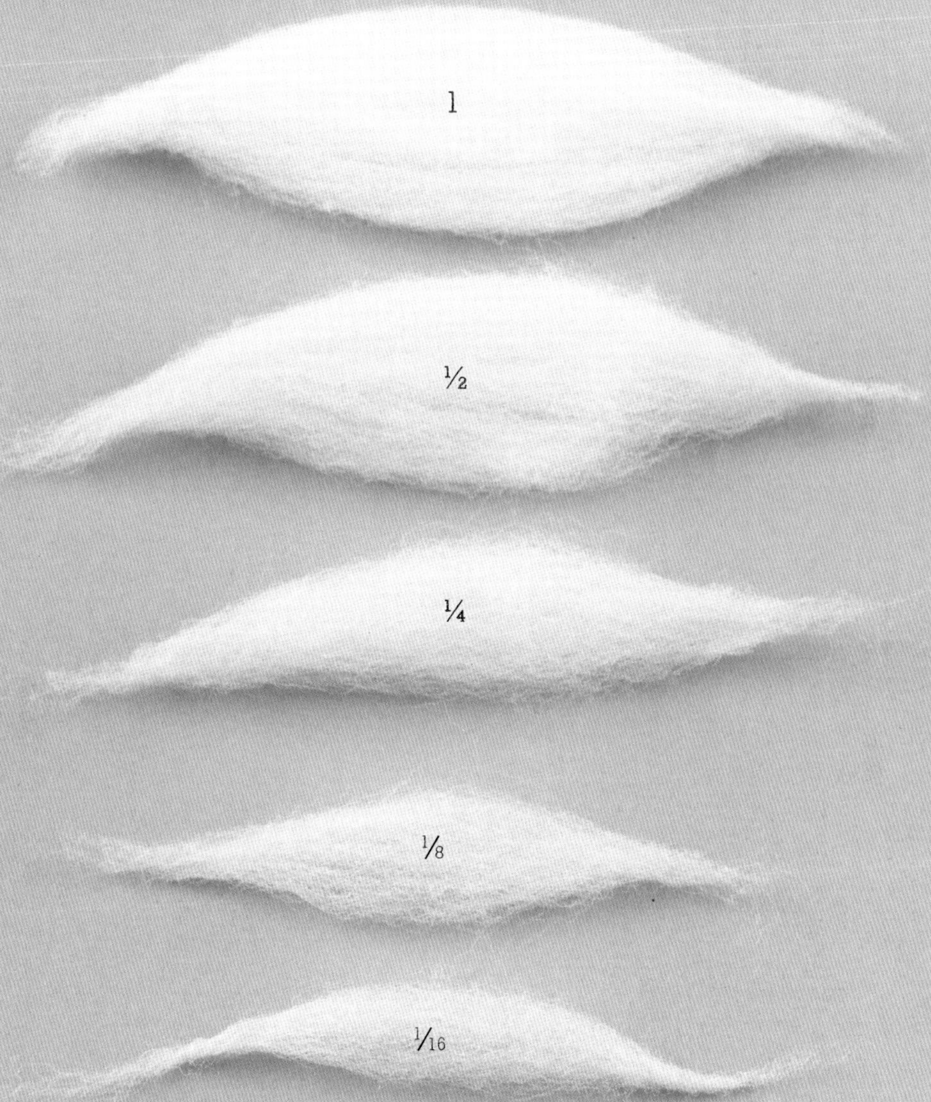

1

½

¼

⅛

1/16

Needle felting

How to hold the felting needle

Felting needles can be fragile. They need to be held correctly to avoid breaking them or hurting yourself. The needle must be kept at the same angle when you withdraw it as when you poke it in: if you put any sideways pressure on it while it is embedded, the tip will snap off.

The barbs of a felting needle are all in the tip or 'working edge', so you do not need to push the needle in any deeper than 2cm (¾in).

Pinch the felting needle between your index finger and thumb. Use your second finger to support the needle, just above the working edge as shown. This allows the end to work properly while avoiding sideways pressure.

22

Needle felting flat shapes

The technique of needle felting flat shapes is essential for making ears, and is at the heart of the craft.

1 Lay your measure of wool on a piece of sponge, and pick up the felting needle. Push the needle through the wool, into the sponge.

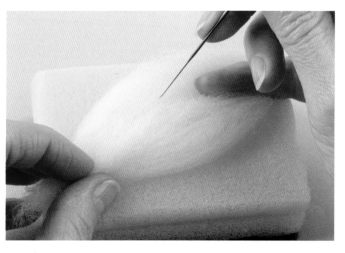

2 Keeping the needle at the same angle, pull it out again. Keeping it at the same angle helps to avoid stress on the needle.

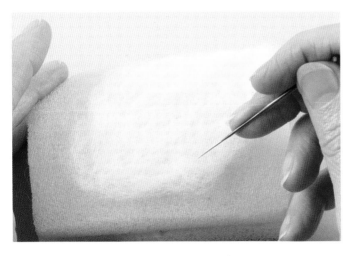

3 Repeat all over the wool using a jabbing action. Aim to 'bounce' the needle in and out of the sponge. This is at the heart of the flat needle-felting technique.

4 The wool will start to adhere to the sponge pad as the fibres and the sponge get felted together, so gently peel the wool away and turn it over every few minutes before continuing.

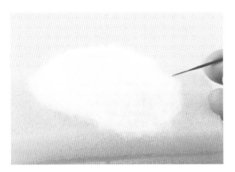

5 To create an edge to the shape, hold the needle at a shallower angle and work it into the edge, working the loose fibres into the rest of the wool. This is called parallel needle felting.

6 As you work, the fibres will bind together more and more tightly, so the shape will gradually become smaller and smaller. Continue working until the felt is the size and shape you want it.

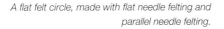

A flat felt circle, made with flat needle felting and parallel needle felting.

Needle felting three-dimensional shapes

Learning how to make simple shapes is fundamental to the art of three-dimensional needle felting.

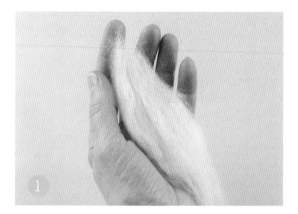

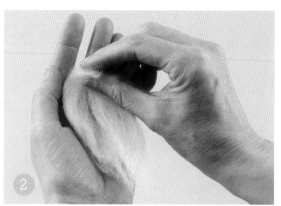

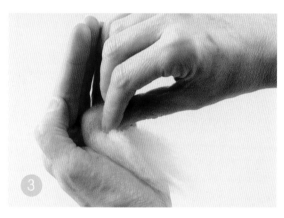

1 Hold the measure in the palm of your hand.

2 Take the end of the wool furthest from you and roll it in towards the palm of your hand.

3 Cup your hand and begin to roll the wool into your palm. As you work, draw wool in from the sides into the centre.

4 Continue until you have a loose ball of wool in your cupped palm.

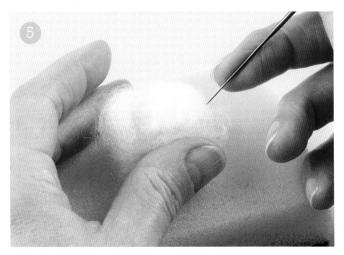

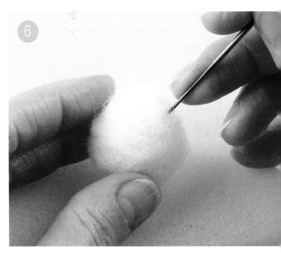

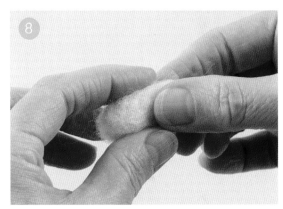

5 Place the ball of wool on the sponge and begin working a standard needle in and out of the ball (rather than into the sponge).

6 Turn the ball as you work, and put the needle in at a different point every time to ensure an even shape.

7 As the fibres begin to felt together and the ball tightens, you can lift it away from the sponge and work it in your hands.

8 While the ball is still fairly loose and spongy, it can either be worked into a tighter ball, or rolled between your fingers into another shape like this capsule.

9 Continue working until the piece is fairly firm, and holds its intended shape. If gently squeezed between your fingers, it should return to its shape.

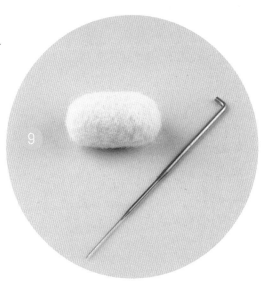

Needle felting on sticks

This technique is used for legs, tails and other similar shapes. If the final step shortens the piece of felt too much, roll it between your hands to lengthen it a little. Similarly, if it ends up too long, you can intentionally shorten it with the fine felting needle.

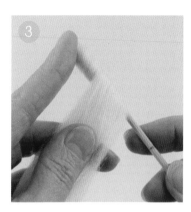

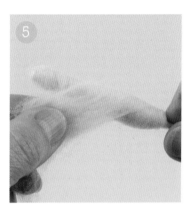

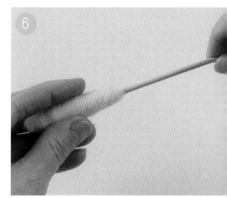

1 Use a pen to mark the measurements on the stick. In this example, we will be using a 6cm (2⅜in) length. Mark the stick all the way round.

2 Draw out the wool a little. Do not worry about the exact length; you simply do not want the wool in a bundled measure.

3 Using one finger to hold the end of the wool on the stick, begin to wrap the length round the stick, turning it and letting the wool wind on gradually at an angle.

4 Wrap the wool evenly round the stick down to the mark.

5 Once you reach the mark, begin to wrap the wool back up the stick until the wool runs out.

6 Twist the stick between your fingers to smooth the wool.

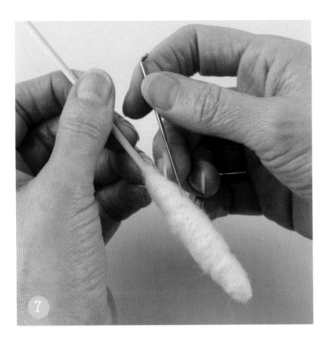

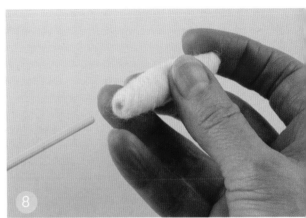

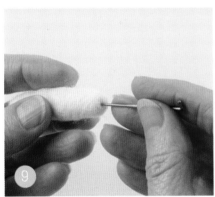

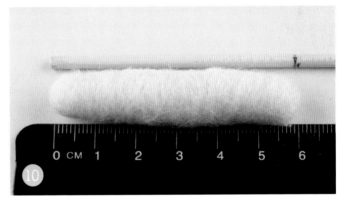

7 Use the fine felting needle to felt the wool around the stick. Change the angle of working every so often so the wool stays within the mark and is worked thoroughly from both ends.

8 Once the wool is firmly felted and is holding itself together, slide it off the stick.

9 Push the standard felting needle into the hole and felt the wool to tighten it from the inside and ensure it holds the shape.

10 Once the felt has tightened, lie the piece down next to your stick (or a ruler) to check the length is correct.

Additional techniques

Implanting

A lot of the parts of the dogs are produced separately, and then combined. Implanting is the process of joining these separate parts seamlessly. Here I am using two different colours to show how the process works.

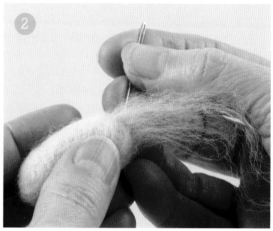

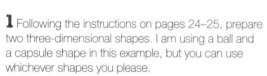

1 Following the instructions on pages 24–25, prepare two three-dimensional shapes. I am using a ball and a capsule shape in this example, but you can use whichever shapes you please.

2 Use an embroidery needle to tease out some loose fibres from one of the pieces (this is typically the smaller of the pieces, though it is not critical).

3 Place the teased-out end on top of the other piece and use the loose fibres to needle felt the pieces together with an in-and-out stabbing motion.

Implanting creates an invisible join.

Repairing holes

Webs of wool (see page 18) can be used to fill gaps or cover holes or crevices in your pieces of felt.

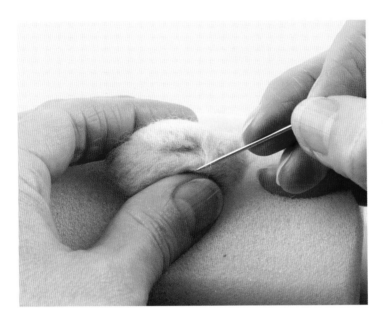

1 Use an embroidery needle to scratch at the hole in your felt to release some loose fibres.

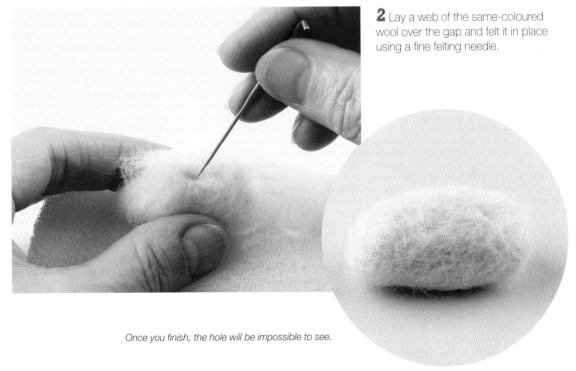

2 Lay a web of the same-coloured wool over the gap and felt it in place using a fine felting needle.

Once you finish, the hole will be impossible to see.

Mixing colours

Wool can be carded together to create a whole range of different colours and muted shades. Lovely graduation can be achieved by adding a little extra light or dark to the wool mix. If you do not have carders, you can use the pull-and-pile technique (see page 16) or pinned dog grooming brushes.

1 Place the two colours of wool on to one of the carders. Aim to work a measure or so of wool at a time.

2 Working in the same direction, repeatedly draw the unloaded carder lightly across the teeth of the loaded carder to thoroughly mix the wools.

3 Once the colours are mixed, hold the carders with the handles pointing in opposite directions and use the top edge of one carder to lift the wool off the other.

COLOUR MIXES

When two or more colours are carded together, the result is a colour mix. Some example colour mixes that are useful for the dogs in this book are shown here.

Charcoal
One part white merino to three parts black merino.

Light vanilla
One part vanilla merino to one part Southdown.

4 Gently roll the wool into a mini batt (see page 9), ready to be used.

5 To make this into measurable lengths, you will need to align the wool, so hold the mini batt in your left hand and gently pull and pile the fibres (see page 16).

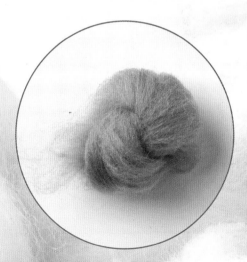

Very dark brown
One part dark brown merino to one part black merino.

Beige
One part beige merino to two parts Southdown.

Making features for your dogs

Bead eyes

After sewing bead eyes in place, check that the hole that goes through the bead is facing to the sides. If the hole is pointing outwards, put the point of an embroidery needle into it to turn the bead into the correct position.

Beads can vary a great deal from supplier to supplier. If the eyes look too small, try the next size up. Likewise, if they appear too large, try the next size down. Keep a good selection of beads from which to choose.

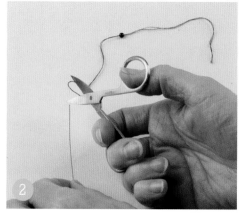

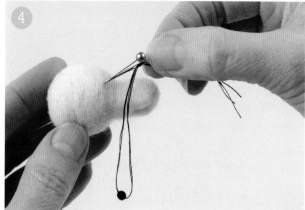

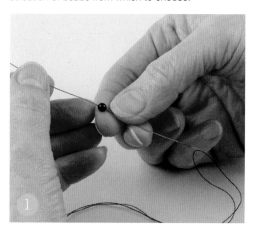

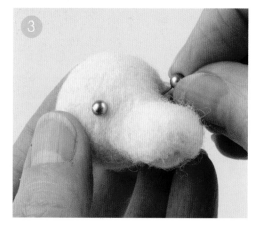

1 Centre a 40cm (15¾in) length of thread on to a beading needle. Run a bead down on to thread the same colour as the bead. This helps hide the thread when you have finished.

2 Centre the bead on the thread, then cut the loop by the needle with a small pair of scissors. This leaves the bead in the middle of a double length of thread. Note that you can use an extra strong thread, in which case you do not need a double thickness.

3 Take your prepared head and use glass-headed pins to mark the positions of the eyes. Place them further out than looks correct; the eyes will be drawn inwards towards each other later.

4 Thread a large-eyed embroidery needle with the double thread and take it down next to the first glass-headed pin. Take the needle right the way through the head, emerging just off-centre at the back of the head.

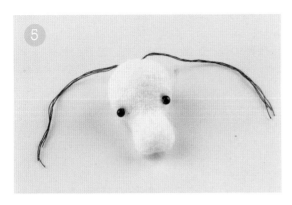

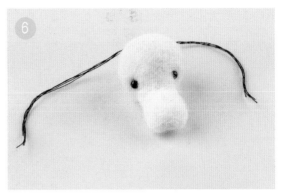

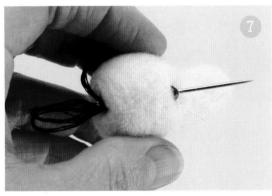

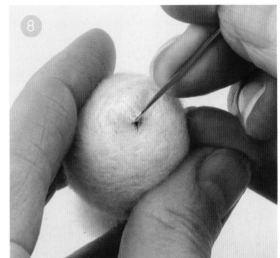

5 Draw the thread through and remove the pin, then repeat with the other eye, making sure to bring the thread out slightly off-centre at the back of the head.

6 Pull the threads tightly, so that the eyes are pulled firmly into the felt of the head. This will distort the felt of the head slightly, sinking them in and giving a more realistic effect. Tie the threads securely into a knot in the centre of the back of the head.

7 Thread the loose ends onto a large-eyed embroidery needle and take them back through the head, emerging as close to one of the eyes as possible, as shown.

8 Pull the thread through and trim it close to the exit point so it disappears back into the felt, then use a web of wool over the little area at the back as though repairing a hole (see page 29).

The finished eyes in place.

Polymer clay eyes

When making these eyes, I suggest you make a selection of different sizes in one go, so that you have a choice when you come to put your dogs together.

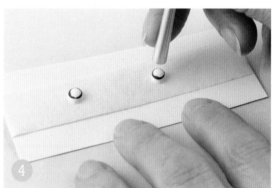

1 Cut out a small rectangle of scrap card and a length of masking tape slightly longer than the card rectangle. Keeping the tape sticky side up, wrap the ends round and secure them in place with two smaller pieces of masking tape. This creates a sticky pad to keep the eyes in place as you paint them. Put this to one side.

2 Place two small balls of white polymer clay on a ceramic tile and use a concave-ended tool to create small domes.

3 Leave the eyes on the tile and bake them, following the manufacturer's instructions. Once baked and cooled, remove the eyes from the tile and gently file down any rough edges using the nail file.

4 Place the eyes on the sticky pad, then prepare a dark mix of raw umber with a little Mars black acrylic paint and dip the end of a slightly smaller concave bead tool into the paint. Place this on the eye, twist and lift away to leave a dark circle. Leave this to dry.

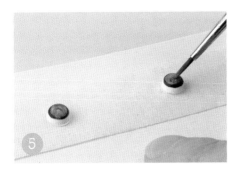

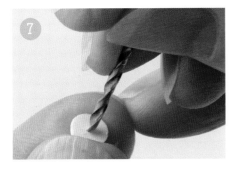

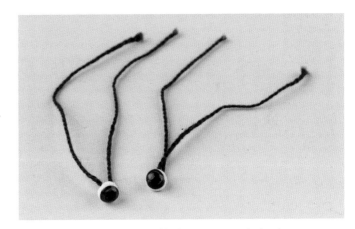

5 Mix raw umber with cadmium yellow deep. Use a small brush to paint this mix within the dark circle. Again, leave to dry.

6 File a cocktail stick down to the right size for the pupil you want, and use this to stamp the centre of the eye with black paint. Allow to dry completely, then paint the eyes with at least two coats of gloss varnish.

7 Cut a 20cm (8in) length of sewing thread and tie a knot in the centre of the thread. Use a 2mm drill bit to drill into the back of the eye to create a small hollow to fit the knot.

8 Add a touch of superglue to the hollow and place the knot of the thread inside. Use a pin to hold it in place until the glue dries.

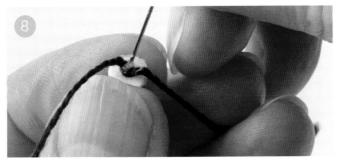

The finished eyes can be attached in the same way as for bead eyes (see pages 32–33).

TIP

Rest the upturned eye on tacky putty to keep it still while gluing. This will also help prevent glue from going on to your fingers as you work.

Making noses

A detailed nose is important to making a realistic finished dog. To get a shiny, moist effect, buff the finished nose with a cloth. Varnish would make it look too shiny.

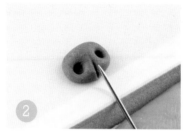

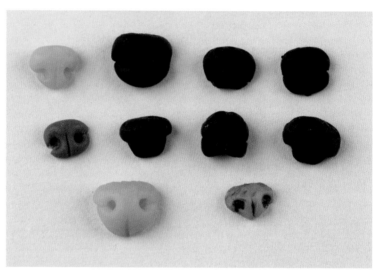

There are many different types of dog noses, so experiment using different coloured clays or with slight variations on the shapes. To get a rounded back on the nose – useful for larger dogs or those with particularly pointy snouts – make the nose on a ball bearing and bake it. Prop the ball bearing on a small lump of polymer clay so that it does not roll while baking.

1 Place a small ball of polymer clay near the edge of a ceramic tile, shape it into an oval, then use the head of a pin to make two indents to represent nostrils.

2 Use the point of the pin to score a line between the nostrils to the bottom of the nose.

3 Use a craft knife at an upward angle to trim a small section away from each side of the nose into the nostrils.

4 Gently pinch the top and bottom together on each side to close the gaps. Leave the nose on the tile and bake it, following the manufacturer's instructions. Once baked and cooled, remove the nose from the tile. If necessary, gently file down any rough edges using the nail file.

Making an H-frame

An H-frame can be used to make a flexible armature for your dog, which will allow you to pose him or her as you wish. If a dog has slender legs, to avoid pipe cleaner fluff poking through the thin layer of wool, trim the fluff from the wires.

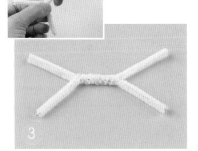

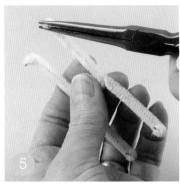

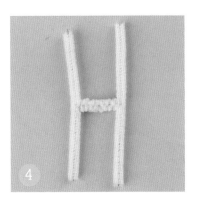

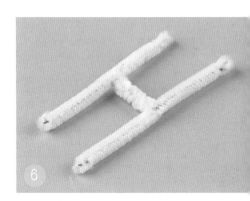

1 Cut two 12cm (4¾in) lengths of pipe cleaner and use a pen to make a mark halfway along each.

2 Lay the lengths across each other and twist them together at the mark.

3 Make three small tight twists to the right of the centre, and four on the left side.

4 Bend the ends up to form right angles as shown. These will be your dog's legs. The shorter ones are the front legs, and the longer ones the rear legs.

5 Lay the H-frame over the template (see below) and use the pen to mark the feet. Bend the wires over using pliers, then check the size. Trim if necessary, using heavy scissors or wire cutters.

6 Use the pliers to flatten the wires against the legs. This prevents the sharp ends poking out of your finished dog.

AN EXAMPLE H-FRAME TEMPLATE

Once you have made your H-frame, lay it over the project template to check the size is correct.

When you bend the wires over, the fluff on the pipe cleaner can make the leg look longer than it is. Ignore the fluff, and measure only the wire core.

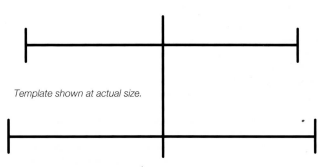

Template shown at actual size.

GST: 2 x 5½"

The dogs

There are a number of ways to construct a needle felted dog. Some people like to complete a head and implant it on afterwards, while others prefer to make the whole sculpture in one piece. I have designed the projects in this book so that you get to create a range of dogs using a variety of different methods.

I recommend you start with the first project and work your way through to the last. Once you have completed all the projects, you will have learnt how to construct a dog sitting, standing and lying, with different facial details and fur effects. Observe and look for what makes a dog unique, then with your new skills you will be able to adjust the shape and coat accordingly to create your own breed of dog.

Each dog is accompanied by a set of templates that allow you to check the parts for the correct size, shape and position. After completing a dog, take a really good look at it from all angles. There will always be final adjustments which can only be made by eye and this is where you decide how your finished dog will look. Liken it to getting a dog ready for a show – that final tweak can make it a winner!

A NOTE ON WOOL

In all of the projects, the amount of wool you will need is listed. This is intended as a guideline, but I always recommend you save a little extra wool for final adjustments and personalisation.

For the projects that are more variable in the amount you might need for the dog, I have rounded up the total measures to the next highest ¼ measure in order to ensure you definitely have all you need for the project.

In any case, it is always a good idea to have lots of spare wool to hand.

REMOVING BROKEN NEEDLES

If the tip of a needle breaks off deep inside a sculpture, push a pin into the hole to mark the place you lost it, then get a pair of tweezers. Remove the marking pin then gently squeeze and bend the sculpture on either side of where the needle broke off. If you are lucky, the end of the needle will show itself and you can pull it out with the tweezers; if you are not, full surgery is required, I'm afraid!

Cocker Spaniel

A cocktail stick will be the starting point from which this tiny doll's house spaniel is born. Such tiny dogs can be difficult to needle felt as fingers have a habit of getting in the way! Using the technique of winding the wool onto sticks makes a fiddly job a little easier and less painful.

If you have never needle felted before, this is a good dog with which to start. If you are a beginner, you may find it helpful to practise the basic techniques on pages 16–31.

Materials

Wool tops: 2 measures of white Southdown; ½ measure of black merino
Felting needles: 36T (standard); 38S (fine); 40S (reverse)
Two small black seed beads
Embroidery needle
Fine beading needle
Strong black thread
Small sharp scissors
Cocktail sticks
Pen
Felting pad

Size

Body length 3.5cm (1⅜in); height 4cm (1½in) to top of head

Difficulty level

Beginner

TEMPLATES FOR THE COCKER SPANIEL

All templates are shown at actual size. Dotted lines indicate the edge of shapes where loose wool (wavy lines) gradually becomes a part of the overall shape.

Stick templates

Place cocktail sticks next to the templates and use a pencil or pen to mark the lengths of the different body parts on the sticks. Check against these templates as you work to ensure the parts are the right size.

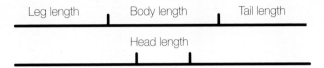

Leg length   Body length   Tail length

Head length

Basic body shape templates

These templates show the basic shapes of the body. Compare the pieces you make with these to ensure the sizes are correct.

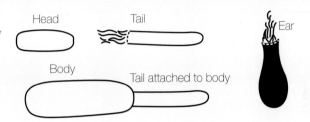

Head   Tail   Ear

Body   Tail attached to body

Basic construction templates

These templates show how the basic parts are assembled and how the shape of the dog is built up.

Reference for details

Facial detail   Patches

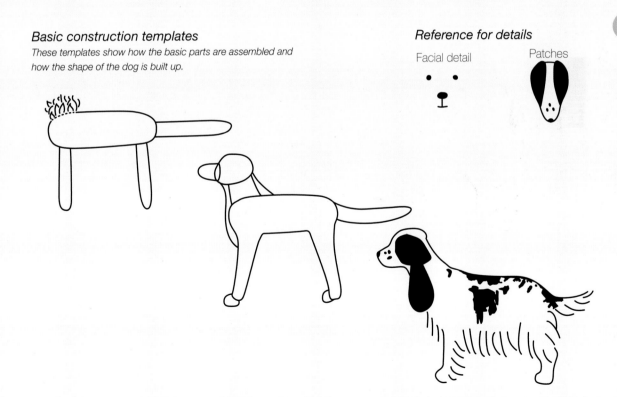

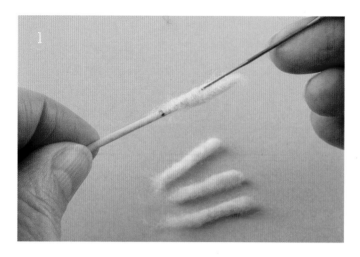

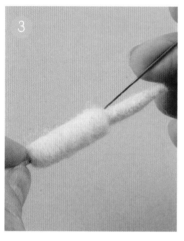

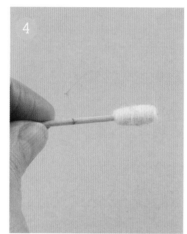

1 Use the felting needle, the cocktail stick marked with the leg length, and the working on sticks technique (see pages 26–27) to make a leg using a ⅟₁₆ measure of white Southdown wool. Once complete, remove the stick and place to one side. Make three more in the same way.

2 Take the cocktail stick marked with the body length, and wind a ½ measure of white Southdown wool onto it between the body marks. Use the same needle and techniques to make a body. Leave this on the stick.

3 Add a tail to the body by winding an ⅛ measure of white Southdown wool onto the stick next to the body and needle felting it into the body. Again, leave this on the stick.

4 Take the cocktail stick marked with the head length, and wind an ⅛ measure of Southdown wool onto the stick between the head marks. Use the same needle and techniques to needle felt the head, then push it all the way to the right end of the stick.

5 Wind a ⅟₁₆ measure of white Southdown wool around half of the head and needle it in place.

6 Remove the head from the stick and place it to one side. Still using the same needle, use the flat needle felting technique to make a teardrop-shaped ear from a ¹⁄₁₆ measure of black merino wool. Parallel needle felt into the edges to make the shape firmer, and leave some loose fibres at the top for later implanting.

7 Make a second in the same way.

8 Referring to the template, use an embroidery needle to scratch at the tops of the legs one at a time, then implant the legs to the body following the instructions on page 28.

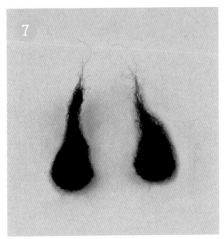

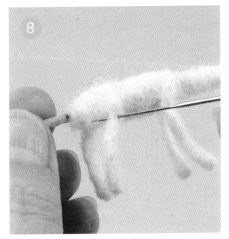

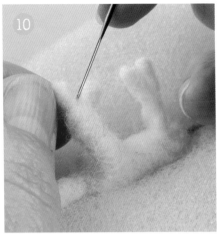

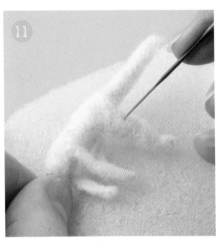

9 Wrap a ¹⁄₁₆ measure of white Southdown around the top part of each leg and needle felt it in place. Attach it loosely using the standard needle, then change to the fine needle. This is because the standard needle can pull the wool about a little too much, while the fine needle will felt it with less disturbance.

10 While the wool is still a little loose, hold the foot, needle felt towards the body and 'tap' in and out rapidly.

11 Once the wool is more secure, change the angle of needle felting to ensure you felt each of the upper legs in place thoroughly.

12 Repeat for the other legs, then pinch the tops of the back legs to flatten them. Needle felt these upper parts of the back legs to fix this shaping.

13 Place a loose ¹⁄₃₂ measure of white Southdown wool on the top of the front of the body and use the fine needle to loosely secure it (see inset). Place the head on top of this, and change to the standard needle to secure the head in place. Work from all angles to ensure a strong bond; even between the front legs as shown.

14 Remove the dog from the stick, wrap a ¹⁄₃₂ measure of white Southdown wool around the neck to thicken and shape it and needle felt it in place with the standard needle. Pull a ¹⁄₁₆ measure of black merino wool apart and pile it so that the fibres go in all directions. Change to the fine needle to attach this to the side of the head, creating a black patch.

15 Needle felt the patch into shape, using the template for reference on size and position; then repeat the process on the other side of the head.

16 Use the standard needle to implant both ears in place.

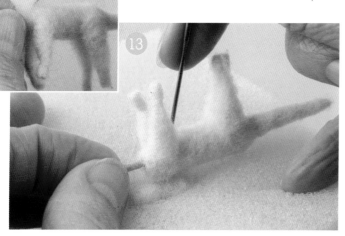

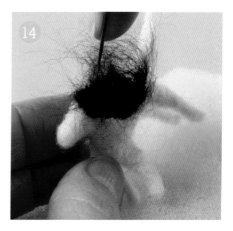

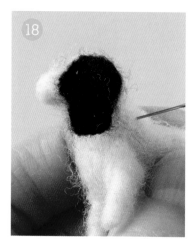

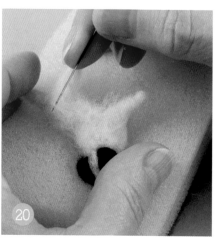

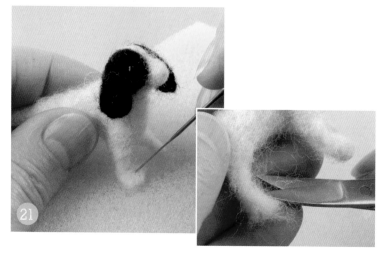

17 Attach two small black seed beads in place as eyes, following the instructions on pages 32–33.

18 Use the fine needle to add a 1/16 measure of white Southdown wool down over the front of the neck and the chest, then add a 1/32 measure of white Southdown wool around the back of the neck.

19 Referring to the template, add shaping to the top of the legs by adding a 1/32 measure of white Southdown wool to each.

20 Bulk up the sides of the body by adding a 1/32 measure of white Southdown wool to each flank. Scratch the fibres over to the sides to blend them smoothly and avoid any gaps.

21 Still using the fine needle, felt a 1/32 measure of white Southdown wool to the front of one of the legs as a foot. Repeat on the other feet, then use fine scissors to trim them to shape (see inset).

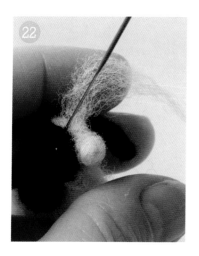

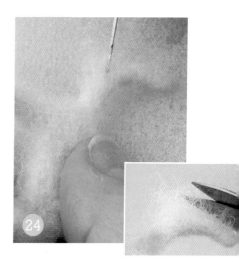

22 Needle a ⅟₃₂ measure of white Southdown wool between the black patches; starting where the muzzle meets the rest of the head and felting it down the neck.

23 Stab the centre of the tail repeatedly using the standard needle. The tail will begin to curl upwards.

24 Next, change to the reverse felting needle and use it to pull out a few strands of wool to represent the longer, fluffier hair on the tail – this type of fur is called 'feathers'. Hold the dog firmly while you do this, and work carefully. Trim the hair to shape using fine scissors (see inset).

25 Use the reverse felting needle and fine scissors to add the feathers on the backs of the legs. Hold the join between the body and the legs while doing this.

26 Make a thread from a ⅟₃₂ measure of white Southdown wool and secure one end between the spaniel's front legs with the fine felting needle. Draw the thread up and secure it a little way along, leaving a little loop of wool. Repeat along the belly of the spaniel.

47

27 Repeat step 26 with new threads between the front and rear legs on both the right and left sides.

28 Trim the loops to create feathers on the belly.

29 Use the fine felting needle to needle felt a nose and mouth, using a tiny amount of black merino wool. Refer to the template for guidance and remember that less is more for this stage – use just a few strands of wool at a time.

30 Check over the whole body and make any adjustments you wish before adding the black markings. To finish, add patches and spots of black merino wool wherever you choose using the fine felting needle.

Labrador Retriever

This little dog, waiting patiently for her walk, is constructed on a basic pipe cleaner H-frame. Once the wool is needle felted onto the H-frame armature you will see the beginnings of a dog. This simple form is called the core and at this stage it can be transformed into many different breeds of dog.

I have chosen to turn this core into a chubby youngster. After the top coat layer is applied, the little dog's face is brought to life. Bead eyes are covered by twisted threads of wool to form lids and her nose and smile are simply needle felted on. An ideal project for a beginner.

Materials

Wool tops: 4½ measures of white Southdown; 3¾ measures of vanilla merino; ¼ measure of beige merino; ¼ measure of black merino

Felting needles: 36T (standard); 38S (fine)

Three 3mm (⅛in) black beads

Embroidery needle

Fine beading needle

Strong black thread

Two 12cm (4¾in) lengths of chenille stick (pipe cleaner)

Wire cutters or strong scissors

Carding brushes

Pliers

Pen

Tracing paper

Felting pad

Size

5cm (2in) long, 7cm (2¾in) high

Difficulty level

Beginner

TEMPLATES FOR THE LABRADOR RETRIEVER

All templates are shown at actual size. Dotted lines indicate the edge of shapes where loose wool (wavy lines) gradually becomes a part of the overall shape.

H-frame template

This H-frame is overlaid with the feet and felt wrapped around in steps 2 and 3 (see page 52) for your reference.

Reference for facial details

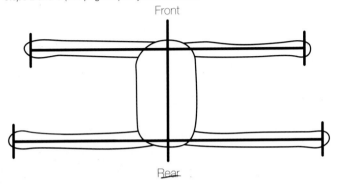

Basic body shape templates

These templates show the basic shapes of the body. Compare the pieces you make with these to ensure the sizes are correct.

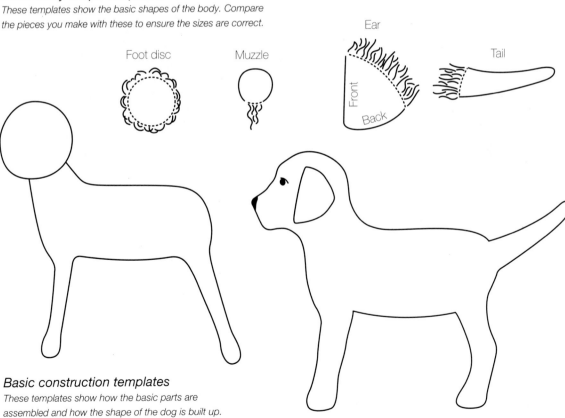

Basic construction templates

These templates show how the basic parts are assembled and how the shape of the dog is built up.

1 Make an H-frame (see page 37) using the chenille stick and the template on page 51, then needle felt a $1/16$ measure of Southdown wool (core wool) into a disc using the fine felting needle. Keep the outside rough and fluffy, and the inside tighter.

2 Make three more discs in the same way, then use the standard needle to felt a disc on to each end of the H-frame, using the thicker centre of each disc as the base.

3 Still using the standard needle, wrap an $1/8$ measure of Southdown wool around each leg and needle felt it in place. Once all the legs are wrapped and felted, wrap and needle felt one complete measure around the body.

4 Make a ball for the head from one measure of Southdown wool. Use an embroidery needle to pull a few threads free and loosely attach it to the body with the implanting technique, making sure to attach it to the front!

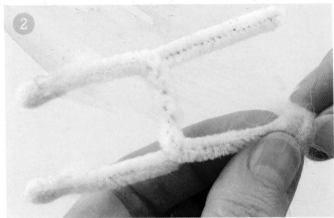

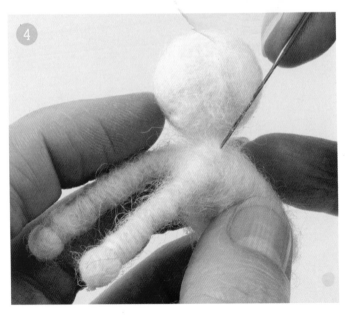

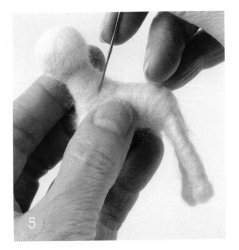

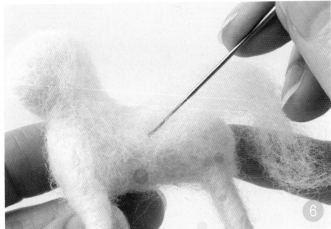

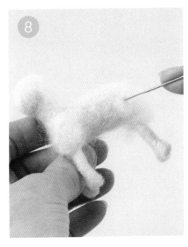

The completed core, ready for the top coat and details to be added.

5 Wind a ¼ measure of Southdown wool around the neck and needle felt it in place. Work from every angle to make sure the head, body and neck are all firmly felted together.

6 Add a ¼ measure of Southdown wool to the chest, another to the bottom and a third across the back to add shaping to the body, using the standard needle for each. Use the templates as reference for shaping.

7 Add a ¼ measure of Southdown wool to the underside and continue adding shaping using the standard needle.

8 Next, use ⅛ measures of Southdown wool for the shaping of the shoulders (front legs) and the tops of the rear legs.

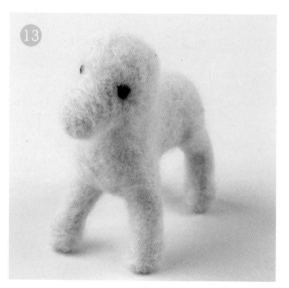

9 Change to the fine needle and cover the core with vanilla merino wool. You are aiming to create an even coat all over. Work in the following order with the amounts shown: head – ½ measure; neck ⅛ measure; back ¼ measure; tummy ¼ measure; chest ¼ measure; bottom ¼ measure; ⅛ measure for each leg; and 1/16 measure for each foot.

10 Bend the rear legs into the correct shape as shown. It is better (and easier) to use your hands for this, rather than the pliers, as you avoid damaging the wool.

11 With the legs correctly positioned, use 1/16 measures of vanilla merino wool to add shaping to each shoulder (front legs) and thigh (rear legs) with the fine needle.

12 Make a ball using an ⅛ measure of vanilla merino wool. Using the standard needle, implant it on the front of the face as the labrador's muzzle. Wrap an ⅛ measure of wool around the point where the muzzle meets the head and needle felt it in place. Scratch the wool between the pieces to help create a smooth blend.

13 Position and attach the beads as eyes using a large-eyed embroidery needle and the technique on pages 32–33.

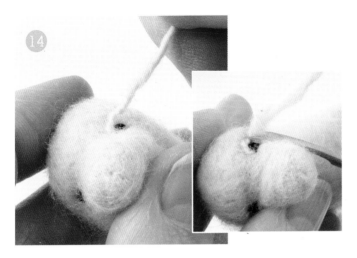

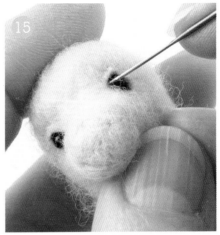

14 Add an eyelid over one eye by making a thread from a 1/32 measure of vanilla merino wool, then using the standard needle to secure it in the corner of the eye. Twist the thread in your fingers, curve it over the bead, then secure it in the other corner of the eye. Trim away the excess (see inset).

15 Make an eyelid on the other eye in the same way, then use a fine felting needle to felt the eyelids in place. Next, needle felt a tiny amount of black merino wool around each eye, underneath the eyelid.

16 Use a fine needle to attach 1/32 measure of black merino wool as the nose. As you felt it in place, work around the edges first, then work in towards the centre. This ensures the bulk of the wool is in the middle, which gives a nice clean edge and gives you more wool in the centre to work with when shaping.

17 Finish shaping the nose, then make a fine thread of black merino wool and attach it under the nose.

18 Still using the fine felting needle add the mouth details by needling black wool thread.

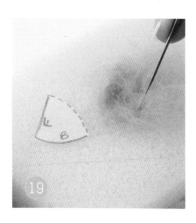

19 Copy the ear pattern onto tracing paper, making sure to mark front and back. Mix ⅛ measure of vanilla and ⅛ measure of beige merino wool and divide into two equal parts. Fluff up an ⅛ measure. Lay it on the pad alongside the pattern and begin to make the shape of the ear using the standard felting needle.

20 Firm up the centre, leaving the dotted line edge fluffy. Place the template on top and carefully trim away any excess felt from the front and back edges.

21 Make a second ear in the same way. Position the first on the dog's head and implant, using the fluffy edge and the standard needle. Start with the ear pointing upwards, and draw both sides in towards the implanting point to shape the ear.

22 Once the ear is attached, fold it over and needle it into place (see inset), then repeat with the second ear. If necessary, you can trim them further once in place using fine scissors.

23 Use an embroidery needle to score a small crease down the crest of the labrador's head. If necessary, you can adjust the shaping of the head using the fine felting needle to get him looking how you want.

24 Make a 2.5cm (1in) long tail on a cocktail stick using a ½ measure of vanilla merino wool and the fine felting needle. Implant it in place to finish. You can add a little hole beneath the tail with the fine felting needle if you would like your labrador to be anatomically correct!

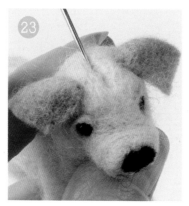

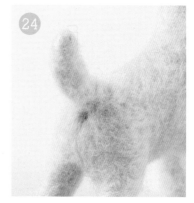

Litter of labradors

This playful group of labradors were all made in the same way as the puppy in the project. The chocolate-coloured labrador was made with dark brown merino wool tops.

Shih Tzu

This show girl shih tzu may look a dainty diva, but she is no lightweight – her body is constructed using a gravel-filled sock! You can add some lavender flowers to the gravel as you make her up to make her smell as pretty as she looks.

The top coat, made of knitting yarn, looks convincingly realistic once unravelled and gently brushed out – though be sure not to stretch the yarn when measuring it in order to ensure you have the correct length. Handmade eyes and nose make her a real show-stopper.

Materials

Wool: Thick grey felting wool yarn, 530cm (209in)

Thick white felting wool yarn, 181cm (72in)

¼ measure of black wool tops

Felting needles: 36T (standard); 38S (fine)

Short grey sock, size ages 7–10 (UK 8–9; Eur 31–36.5; US 12.5–3.5)

Wadding/batting, 1.5cm (½in) thick

Sewing thread

Thick thread

Embroidery needle

Curved needle (optional)

Claw tool

Glass-headed pins

Sharp scissors

Aquarium gravel 15g (½oz)

Lavender flowers (optional)

Sharp scissors

Tape measure

Foam pad

Polymer clay nose (see page 36)

Two polymer clay eyes (see page 34–35)

Glue: superglue, tacky white glue

Scrap card and masking tape

Wooden skewer or cocktail stick

Nail file

Drill bit size 2mm (¹⁄₁₆in)

Fine needle or blade

Carding brushes

Size
10cm (4in) long, 10cm (4in)high

Difficulty level
Average

TEMPLATES FOR THE SHIH TZU

All templates are shown at actual size.

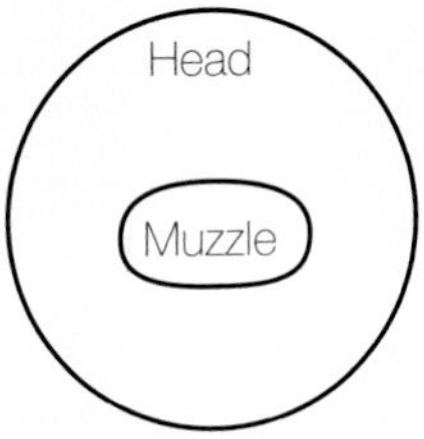

Head

Muzzle

Basic body shape templates

These templates show the basic shapes of the body. Dashed lines indicate underlying shapes beneath surface layer (solid lines).

Top of body

Bottom of body

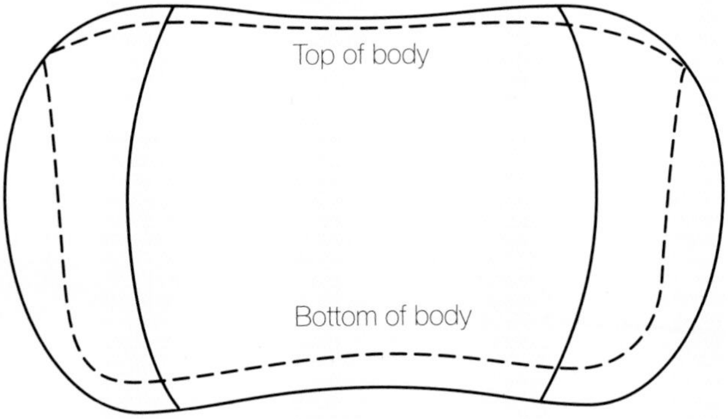

Wadding template

The solid line indicates the half size template; the dashed line the full size.

Fold line

Fold line

Reference for facial details

Eye

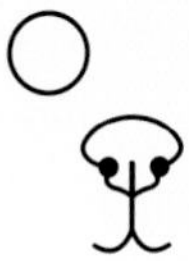

Nose and mouth

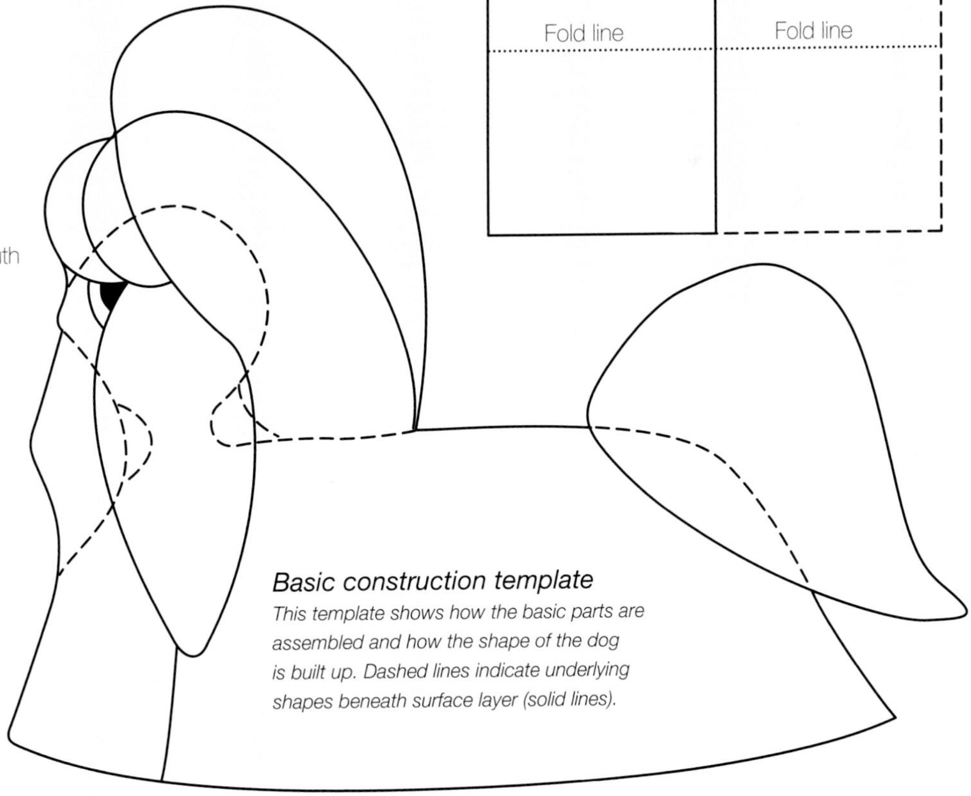

Basic construction template

This template shows how the basic parts are assembled and how the shape of the dog is built up. Dashed lines indicate underlying shapes beneath surface layer (solid lines).

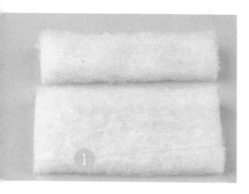

1 Using the wadding/batting template for reference, cut out one full-size piece of wadding and one half-size piece.

2 Fold the full-size piece over along the pocket fold (see template) to form a flat sausage and secure it with pins.

3 Oversew the ends using white thread and an embroidery needle. This forms a pocket.

4 Fill the pocket with gravel. You can add lavender if you wish.

5 Wrap the top of the wadding/batting over the pocket and stitch it closed with the needle and thread to make a parcel.

6 Place the parcel on top of the half-sized piece of wadding/batting (see inset), then wrap the half-sized piece tightly round over the top of the parcel and stitch it closed.

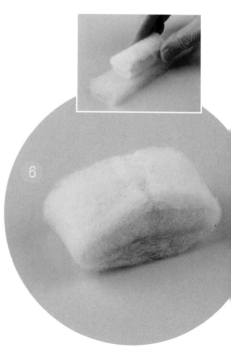
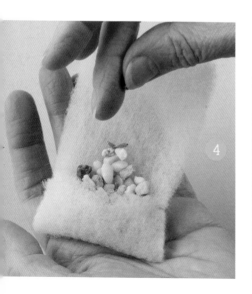
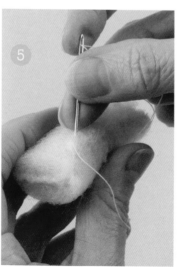

7 Turn the sock inside out, and place the parcel inside at the toe end. Fold and roll the parcel over inside the sock, keeping it taut as you gradually draw your hand out of the sock.

8 At the end, fold over the top and pull the elasticated seam back over into position to keep it together.

9 Pin a 230cm (90½in) length of thick grey wool 1.5cm (½in) from one end of the parcel. Wrap the wool around twelve times, finishing 1.5cm (½in) from the other end. As you work, push the wool strands together to ensure full coverage. Pin it in place and do not cut the wool.

10 Use the embroidery needle and thread to stitch along the top of the body to hold the wool securely in place on the parcel.

11 Take the free end of the wool and pin it to the bottom of the parcel, two wraps in, as shown.

12 Turn the wool and take it up the back of the parcel, then pin it to the top, two wraps in. Pin the wool alternately at the top and bottom four times at the top, four at the bottom.

13 Secure the wool in place with the embroidery needle and thread, removing the pins from the top as you go. Leave the pins in the bottom for the moment. If you have any excess wool, take it to the pins at the bottom and trim it off.

14 Repeat the process at the front of the parcel using a 70cm (27½in) length of white wool (see inset). When you are sure that all the wool is securely attached, remove the pins at the bottom. Cut each of the loops – right at the centre – at the front and back, then slide a stick through the yarn underneath. Using the stick to ensure you do not cut the sock, cut right down the centre of the loops.

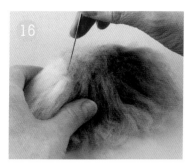

15 Gently unravel and tease apart the released strands of wool one by one, using your fingers and the claw tool. Collect the brushings of wool that the claw takes off the strands as you work round.

16 Felt the spare brushings across the top of the body using the standard felting needle to cover the stitching.

17 Gently squeeze the body into shape, then turn the dog over and trim the hair to length using the scissors. Be careful not to cut the hair too short – it can be trimmed later, but it can not be easily lengthened.

18 Cut a 30cm (11¾in) length of grey yarn and use the carding brushes to card it into loose wool (see inset). Cut a 70cm (27½in) length of grey wool and wind it into a ball.

19 Wrap the loose wool around the ball and use the fine felting needle to turn it into a felt ball.

20 Use an embroidery needle to draw out some strands of wool from the ball, and use the standard felting needle to implant the ball in place as the head.

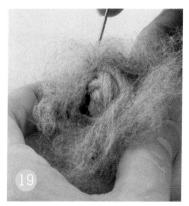

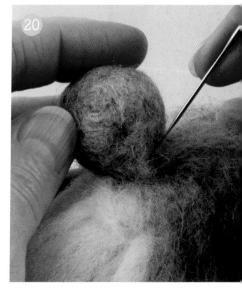

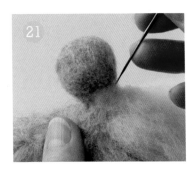

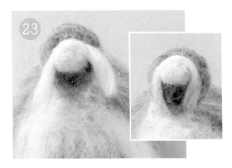

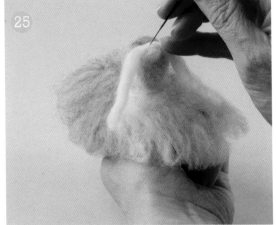

21 Card a 15cm (6in) length of grey yarn into loose wool and needle felt it in place between the head and body as the back of the neck, then do the same with a 15cm (6in) length of white yarn as the front of the neck.

22 Card a 6cm (2⅜in) length of white yarn into loose wool, then use the standard felting needle to attach it to the front of the face. Once secured, change to the fine felting needle and shape it into the shih tzu's muzzle.

23 Cut a 6cm (2⅜in) length of white yarn. Do not card this, but instead needle felt it directly above and all the way down each side of the muzzle (see inset).

24 Cut another 6cm (2⅜in) length of white yarn, card it into loose wool and fill the area below the muzzle and between the lines.

25 Cut a 14cm (5½in) length of white yarn. Do not card this, but instead secure it directly above the muzzle using the fine felting needle, so that it hangs evenly on both sides like a moustache.

Facial detail diagrams

These stages can be hard to follow owing to the need to keep the wool blended smoothly. These diagrams, and the ones on the opposite page, help to show how to build up this dog's distinctive facial details.

23

Front

24
Front

25

Side

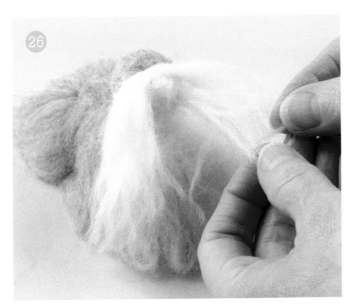

26 Lift one side of the moustache and implant the end of an 8cm (3⅛in) strand of white yarn directly below it, using the standard felting needle. Repeat on the other side with a second strand of wool, then gently unravel both strands and the strands of the 'moustache'. This forms the shih tzu's distinctive beard.

27 For the topknot, cut a 20cm (7⅞in) length of white yarn, fold it in half and attach the centre just above the top of the muzzle using the standard felting needle.

28 In the same way, attach two 20cm (7⅞in) lengths of grey wool horizontally just above the white strand, as shown. These lengths will become the brows and part of the topknot.

26   27 + 28

Side   Front

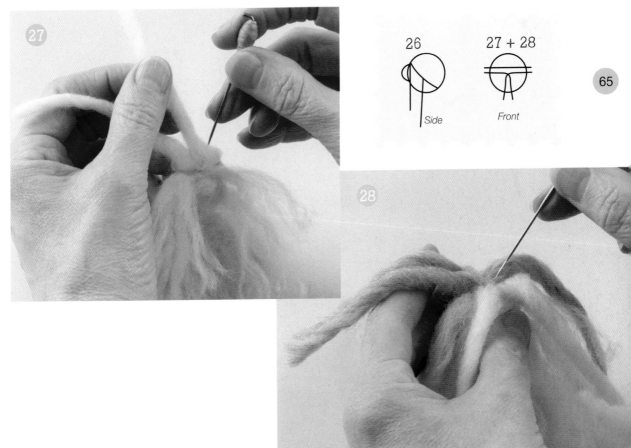

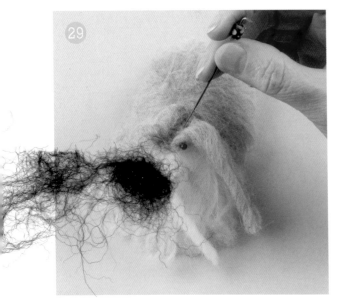

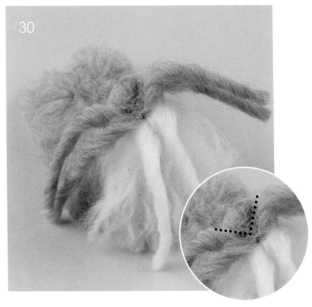

29 Place a pin at the point between where the white and grey strands are attached to temporarily mark the eye's position. Fold the grey strands down and needle across the top of the eye, at an upward-slanting angle.

30 Repeat on the other side, then remove the temporary pins. When both lines are felted, a chevron shape (highlighted in the inset) will be formed.

31 Unravel the grey and white strands, being careful to keep them separate both from each other and the beard. Next, lift the unravelled strands up, with the white part forming the front of the topknot and the grey part the sides and back.

32 Use a short length of fine wire or thread to tie the topknot into a bunch, approximately halfway up.

33 Attach the two large polymer clay eyes as shown.

34 Card a fair amount of grey yarn into loose wool and use it to build up the head behind the eyes, felting it in place using the fine needle. Continue to add small amounts of wool until the eyes are facing forward symmetrically, as shown.

35 Slip an embroidery needle behind the topknot above the eye and tease the wool forwards to create the brow.

36 Scratch the back of the polymer clay nose with the point of a needle to roughen it, then apply fast-acting white glue to the back and fix it on the muzzle.

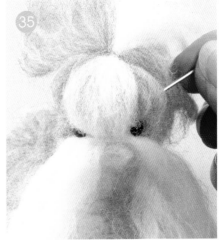

37 Holding the nose in place while you work, attach a 6cm (2⅜in) length of white yarn just above and behind the nose, using the fine felting needle. Use a needle to unravel the strands and blend it into the rest of the beard.

38 Card a tiny amount of grey yarn into loose wool and felt it in place on the muzzle beneath the nose using the fine felting needle. Use a tiny amount of black wool to needle a black line for the mouth, and push a few of the black mouth fibres up towards the nose.

39 Cut three 10cm (4in) lengths of grey yarn, fray the ends, and lift the topknot. Use the standard felting needle to secure them under the topknot.

40 Once secured, felt the other ends into the neck. This will help to bulk up the head and make it more sturdy.

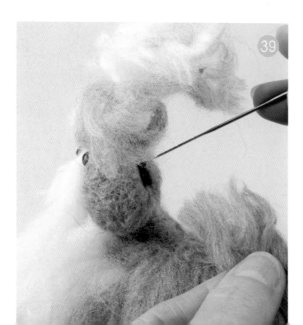

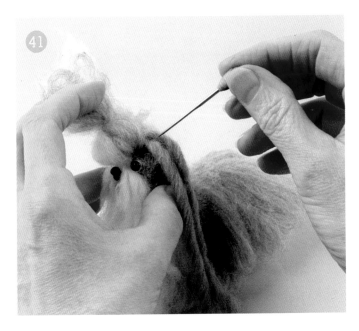

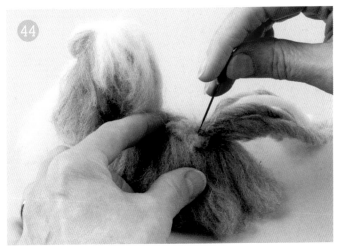

41 Cut a 20cm (7⅞in) length of grey wool, fold it in half, and use the standard felting needle to secure it in place as the ear.

42 Unravel the wool, curl it round as shown and use the standard felting needle to secure the other end into the 'skirt' of fur, just under the shih tzu's neck.

43 Repeat on the other side for the second ear, then arrange the topknot to your satisfaction, taking it over the ears.

44 Cut four 15cm (6in) lengths of grey and two 15cm lengths of white wool, arrange the grey lengths around the white and fray approximately 2.5cm (1in) from the end using a claw tool. Leaving 1cm (½in) of loose wool, use the standard felting needle to needle the frayed part firmly together, then use the loose wool to attach it on the back of the dog as the tail.

45 Once securely attached at the base, unravel the tail and arrange it as shown. Lightly tack it in place here and there using the standard felting needle, if necessary.

46 Use scissors to trim the tail into a point. This will leave a little of the white showing at the tip; then make any other adjustments you wish. You may want to add a little extra wool here or there to thicken or balance the coat.

47 To finish, use the claw tool and your fingers to shape the tail as shown, and add a small bow at the base of the topknot.

Lady on red

This shih tzu looks every bit the lady. She will get plenty of attention if you use her as an elegant paper weight.

Border Terrier

Merino wool alone is rather too flat for this border terrier's textured coat. Adding crimpy Southdown to a wool mix not only makes it look more natural; it also makes it easier to needle felt. The reverse needle does a good job of creating a two-tone blush that would take hours to achieve with a standard felting needle. Small bead eyes and a simple needle-felted nose are all that is required to finish off his cheeky otter-like head.

Materials

Wool tops: 4¼ measures of white Southdown; 2 measures of beige merino; ½ measure of black merino; ¼ measure of dark brown merino

Felting needles: 36T (standard); 38S (fine), 40S (reverse)

Two 3mm (⅛in) black beads

Two 12cm (4¾in) lengths of chenille stick (pipe cleaner)

Embroidery needle

Fine beading needle

Strong black thread

Two 12cm (4¾in) lengths of chenille stick (pipe cleaner)

Wire cutters or strong scissors

Small sharp scissors

Carding brushes

Pliers

Pen

Tracing paper

Pencil

Cocktail stick

Felting pad

Size

5cm (2in) long, 6.5cm (2½in) high

Difficulty level

Average

TEMPLATES FOR THE BORDER TERRIER

All templates are shown at actual size. Dotted lines indicate the edge of shapes where loose wool (wavy lines) gradually becomes a part of the overall shape.

Tail stick template

Tail length

H-frame template

Front

Rear

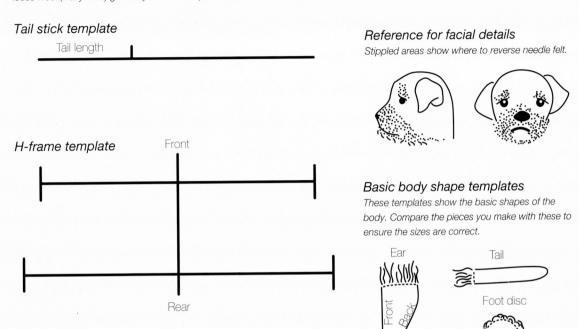

Reference for facial details

Stippled areas show where to reverse needle felt.

Basic body shape templates

These templates show the basic shapes of the body. Compare the pieces you make with these to ensure the sizes are correct.

Ear

Front

Back

Tail

Foot disc

Basic construction templates

These templates show how the basic parts are assembled and how the shape of the dog is built up.

Core

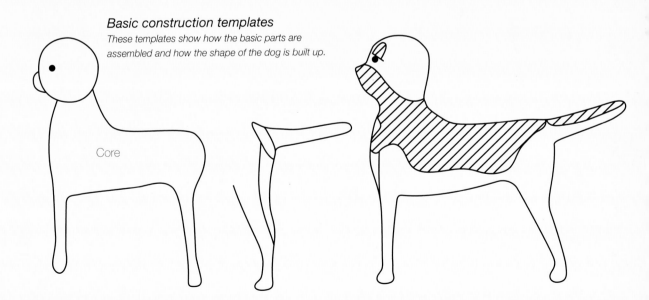

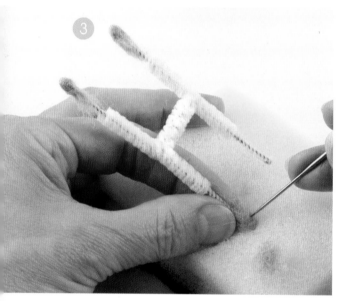

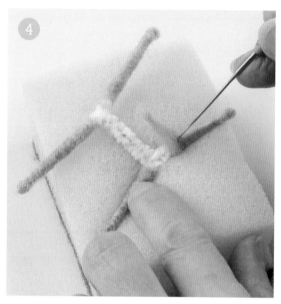

1 Make an H-frame (see page 37) using the lengths of chenille stick and the template on page 73, then trim away the fluff from the bottom half of each leg using scissors.

2 Card together four measures of Southdown wool tops with two measures of beige merino wool tops. Prepare single measures to divide and use as required throughout the project. This carded wool is referred to as 'beige mix' throughout. Needle felt a $\frac{1}{32}$ measure of the beige mix into a disc using the fine felting needle. Keep the outside rough and fluffy, and the inside tighter.

3 Make four discs in total, then use the fine needle to felt one disc on to each foot of the H-frame, using the thicker centre as the base for each foot.

4 Wrap and needle felt an $\frac{1}{8}$ measure of the beige mix wool around each leg. Check all four legs are the same size. If not, add tiny amounts of loose wool to even them up.

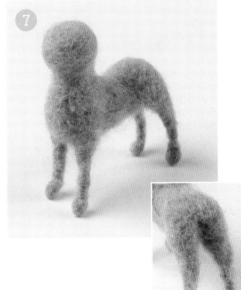

5 Wrap a whole measure of the beige mix wool round the body and needle felt it in place in the same way as the legs. Make a ball for the head using a ½ measure of the beige mix wool, and implant it at the front of the body (double-check the length of the legs to ensure you are fixing it in the right place).

6 Referring to the templates for shaping, begin to bulk up the body by needle felting a ¼ measure of the beige mix wool around the neck between the head and the body; a ¼ measure on the front of the chest; and an ⅛ measure on the bottom. Use the standard felting needle to secure the wool, and change to the fine felting needle to felt the area.

7 With the same needles and techniques, add an ⅛ measure on the underside of the body, with more towards the chest end; then add ⅛ measures to the top of each leg on the shoulders (front legs) and thighs (rear legs). Border terriers have quite straight rear legs, so you need to add a little more muscle to the haunches of the back rear legs. Use a ¹⁄₁₆ measure of the beige mix wool to build up the muscle, and then make an indentation where the bottom goes in, as shown in the inset.

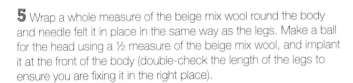

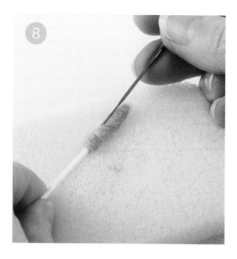

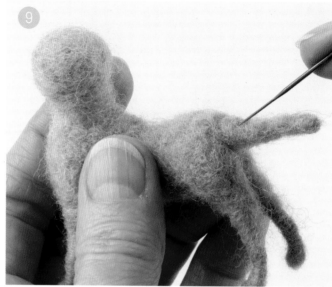

8 Make a 2.5cm (1in) tail using the needle felting on sticks technique (see pages 26–27), the template on page 73, a cocktail stick, an ⅛ measure of the beige mix wool and the fine felting needle.

9 Fray approximately 0.5cm (¼in) of loose wool at the end and implant it onto the body using the standard felting needle. Wrap a ¹⁄₃₂ measure of the beige mix wool around the tail where it joins the body. Use the fine felting needle to blend the measure in and mask the join.

10 Use a ¹⁄₃₂ measure of the beige mix wool and the fine felting needle to create a muzzle. This can be added to the front or side of the head, depending on which way you would like the dog to face.

11 Position and attach two 3mm (⅛in) beads as eyes, following the instructions on pages 32–33. Use an ⅛ measure of loose beige mix wool with the fine felting needle to cover the eye threads at the back of the head, and to reshape the head.

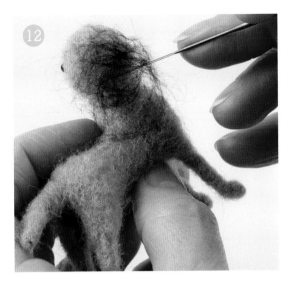

12 Take an ⅛ measure of black merino wool. Using the fine felting needle, begin to develop the markings on the terrier's coat. For light markings such as on the back of the head, pull a few fibres from the ⅛ measure and use them to create a fine web of loose wool before felting it in place.

13 For darker markings, use more loose wool. Build up the coat in sections across the back and side.

14 Once the wool is established in a blocky shape, soften the edges by drawing them out with the tip of an embroidery needle, then use the fine felting needle to felt the strands in.

15 A $\frac{1}{16}$ measure of black merino wool will provide enough loose wool for you to pattern the front of the chest and the neck in the same way. Use a $\frac{1}{32}$ measure for the top of the tail and for the indentation below the tail; and a $\frac{1}{16}$ measure for the muzzle and eyebrow.

16 Use a $\frac{1}{16}$ measure of white Southdown wool for the chest markings, implanting the wool with the fine felting needle.

17 Use the reverse felting needle to needle all over the chest and back markings. Work lightly to avoid taking out too much wool.

18 Change to the fine felting needle and work back over the same area to produce the distinctive effect of the border terrier's fur. Do not flatten the fur completely; aim for a slightly wiry appearance. Draw a few threads across to blend at the edges of the black markings to ensure a natural-looking blend between the lighter and darker areas.

19 Use a fine reverse felting needle to draw out the fur on the other black areas (see inset) including the back of the head, then change to a fine felting needle to work over the same areas.

20 Use a $\frac{1}{32}$ measure of black merino wool with the fine felting needle to add a nose, then use a $\frac{1}{32}$ measure of white Southdown wool to create a chin with a white flash at the bottom of the muzzle. Needle around the white area but leave the centre standing proud.

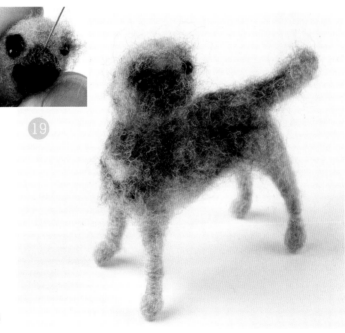

21 Still using the fine felting needle, use a few spare threads of loose black merino wool to add a mouth line across the top of the white flash, then run a dark eyelid line across the top of the eyes. Slant them downwards to the sides to get the distinctive border terrier expression. At this point, you can use the tip of an embroidery needle to draw out the muzzle area and reshape the head if necessary.

22 Card a ⅟₃₂ measure of black merino and a ⅟₃₂ measure of dark brown merino together to make a ⅟₁₆ measure of very dark brown wool. Use this to needle felt two ears in the shape of the template on page 73. Parallel felt the front and back edges of each ear, and leave the remaining edge on each loose. Use the loose wool and the standard felting needle to implant the ear pointing slightly up and back (see inset). Once implanted, repeatedly tap the ear in the middle, near where it joins the head. This will cause it to curl inwards into a cupped shape.

23 Tidy up the back of the ear, then repeat with the second ear. Score a line down the centre line of the head using an embroidery needle to create a crease, then fluff the fur up a little with the tip of the needle to finish.

Ready to go!

Pulling more light-coloured wool to the surface has made the facial details more visible in the foreground terrier. Above the eyes, light wool is reverse felted out then lightly needle felted back in; while on the muzzle I reverse felted out some light wool, then trimmed it with small scissors.

Once these optional changes are made, why not make a little neckerchief for your terrier? Simply soak a tiny square of fabric in watered-down white glue, then fold it over a collar made from cord. Use jewellery findings to make a fastening. Lay the wet neckerchief over a small dome-shaped object to dry, and finish it off with a tiny button.

Standard Poodle

This elegant larger-scale dog was made by winding wool onto a skewer to form basic parts that are then sculpted together. Once the basic body is shaped, a twisted thread top coat is applied to give the desired curly effect. Needling a curly coat from straight wool is a skill well worth learning, even though it is rather time-consuming. If you do not want to cover the whole body in curls, you could pretend your dog has just had a short body clip, leaving only curly top knot and legs!

Materials

Wool tops: 32 measures of white Southdown; 1 measure of black wool

Felting needles: 36T (standard); 38S (fine)

Two 4mm (¼in) black beads

Embroidery needle

Fine beading needle

Strong black thread

Small sharp scissors

Round wooden skewer

Pen

Felting pad

Polymer clay nose (see page 36)

Size

14cm (5½in) from the top of the head to the toes

Difficulty level

Average

TEMPLATES FOR THE
STANDARD POODLE

All templates are shown at actual size.

Tail (pre-shaping)

Shaped tail

Stick template

All measurements on this template should be made from the left-hand end to the appropriate mark.

Back leg   Front leg   Body

Muzzle

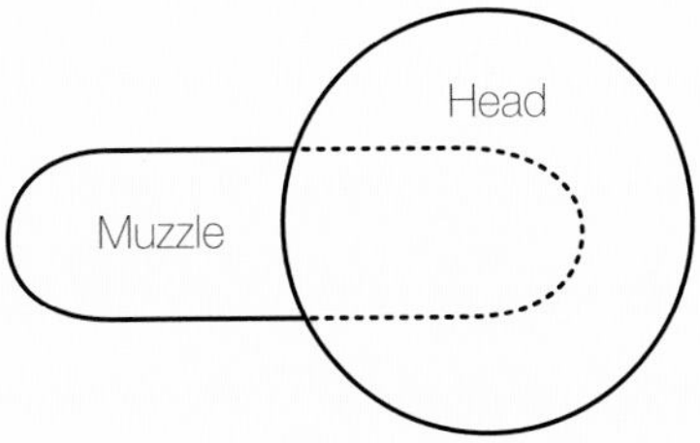

Head

Muzzle

Basic body shape templates

Compare the pieces you make with these to ensure the sizes are correct. Dotted lines indicate areas hidden when implanted or covered with top-coat wool.

Basic construction template

This template shows how the basic parts are assembled. Note that this template shows the leg and back discs leaning at the angles in which they should be assembled.

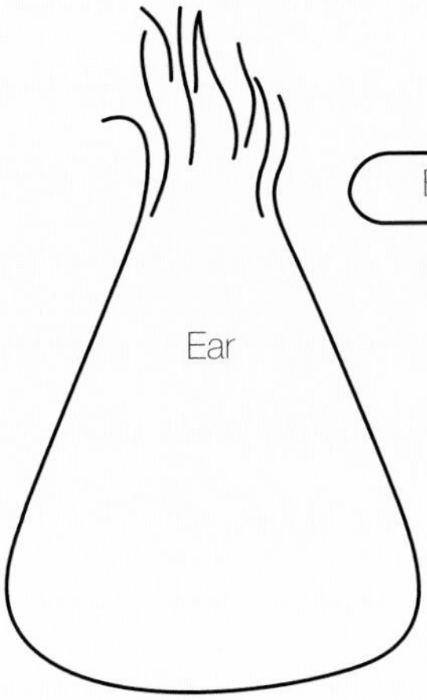

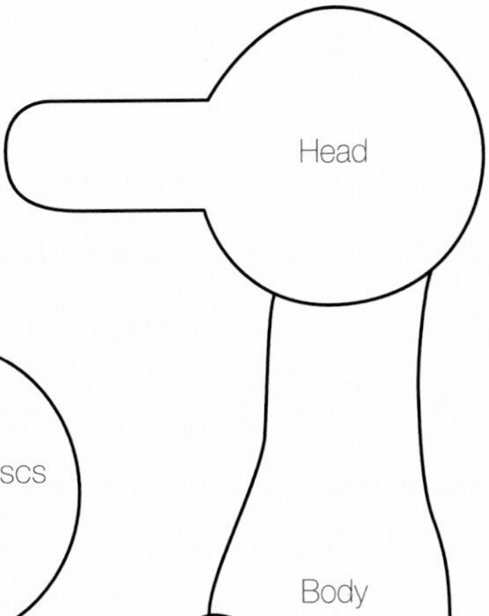

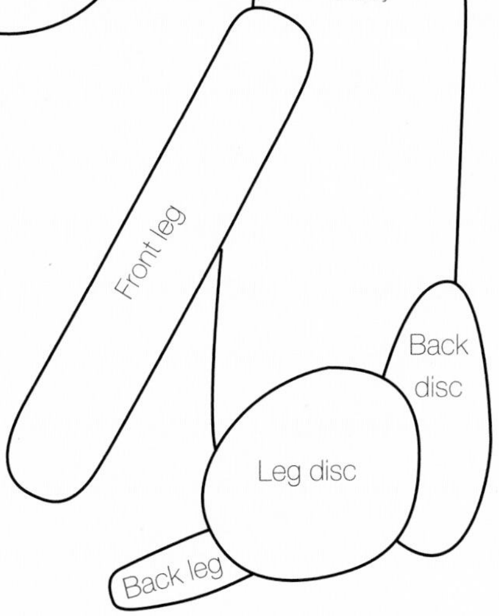

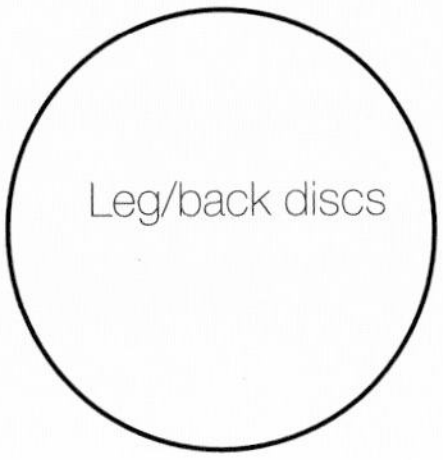

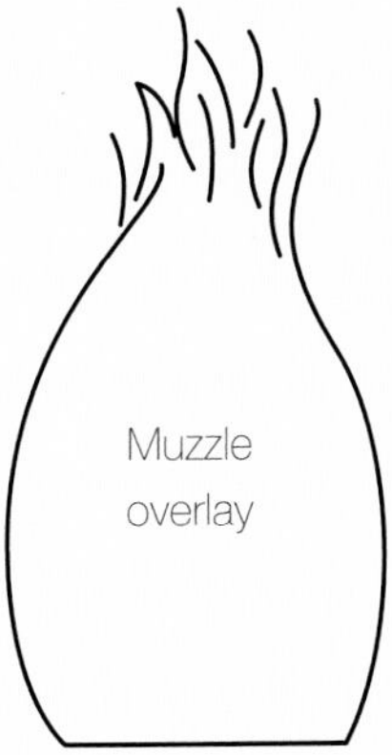

Head

Toe

Back leg

Ear

Body

Leg/back discs

Body

Front leg

Muzzle
overlay

Back
disc

Leg disc

Back leg

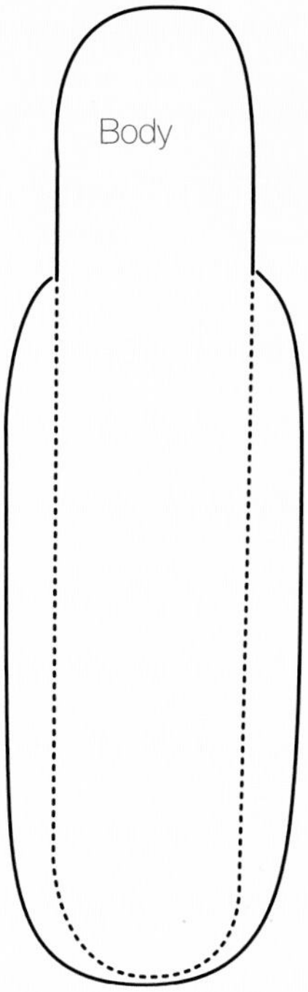

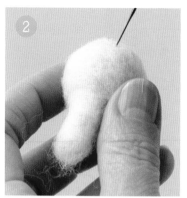

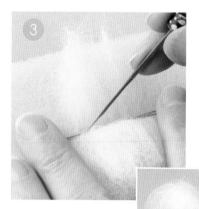

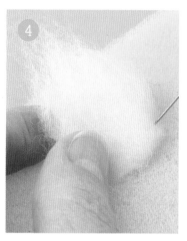

1 Using the needle felting on sticks technique on pages 26–27, and the standard felting needle, work a whole measure of white wool into a 4cm (1½in) cylinder for the muzzle. Refer to the template on page 83. Change to the fine felting needle once the wool is starting to hold.

2 Wrap two whole measures of white wool around the top half of the cylinder while it is still on the skewer and use the standard felting needle to establish a ball that is attached to the cylinder. Once it is holding its shape, remove the piece from the skewer and tighten the ball using the fine felting needle.

3 Pull and pile a ¼ measure of white wool until the bulk of the wool is 10cm (4in) long. Hold the wool on your felting pad and needle a line across the centre using an embroidery needle as a guide. This line is on the lower side.

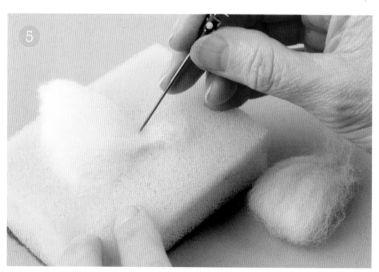

4 Lift the wool off the pad and fold it so the upper side is outwards, then replace it on the pad and use the fine felting needle to needle the ends of the line inwards until it measures 2cm (¾in) across. This is the muzzle overlay.

5 Pull and pile a ½ measure of white wool until it is 9cm (3½in) long, then fold it over and needle the unfolded ends together lightly using the fine felting needle. This is an ear. Make a second in the same way.

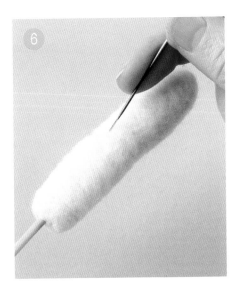

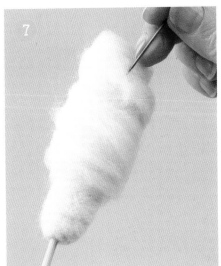

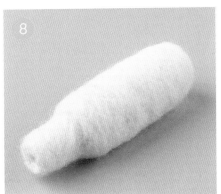

6 To make the body cylinder, wind five whole measures of white wool around the skewer up to a 9cm (3½in) mark and needle using the stick technique as for the muzzle in step 1.

7 Wrap three measures of white wool around the body cylinder, leaving a 2.5cm (1in) area clear for the neck, then begin to needle these with the standard felting needle.

8 Change to the fine felting needle to finish the body wrap, then remove the body from the skewer.

9 Make three 3cm (1⅛in) balls of white wool, each from a single measure, then use the standard felting needle to felt them into discs for the thighs and lower back (refer to the leg disc template for the exact size).

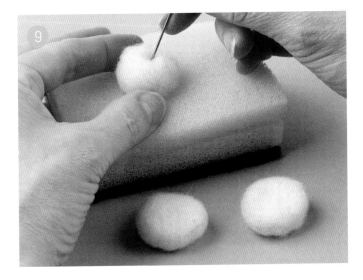

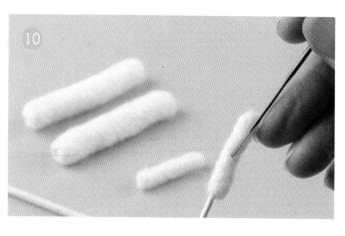

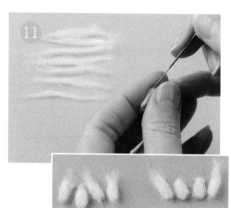

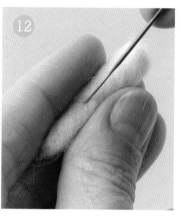

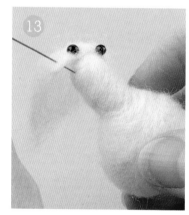

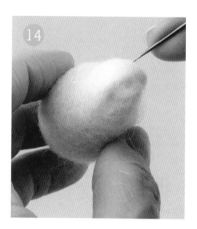

10 Make two 6cm (2⅜in) long front legs using the stick technique with a skewer and 1½ measures each; then make two 3cm (1⅛in) back legs in the same way using a cocktail stick and a ¼ measure each. As before, establish the wool with the standard needle then change to the fine needle to finish.

11 Divide an ⅛ measure into eight. Needle each piece on the pad until the fibres hold together, then roll them between your fingers before tightening them into eight tiny toes with the fine felting needle (see inset).

12 Make a 4cm (1½in) tail with the stick technique using a skewer and a ½ measure of white wool. Remove it from the skewer, roll pinch and needle one end to make it slightly pointed. This completes the basic parts – put them all safely to one side.

13 Place the needled fold of the muzzle overlay on the front of the extended part of the head (the muzzle) and pin it in place.

14 Use the standard felting needle to needle the wool into the top and the sides of the muzzle while pushing in the front of the muzzle with your thumb.

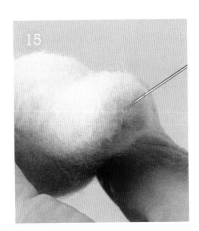

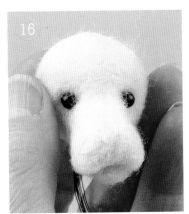

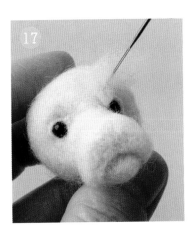

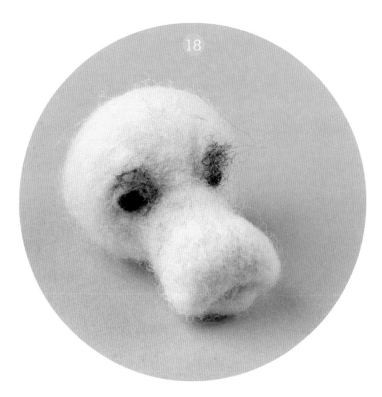

15 Change to the fine felting needle and form the overlay into the shape of the mouth and upper 'lip' of the poodle. Add an ⅛ measure of white wool to the top front to slightly square off the front and establish the shape of the nose.

16 Use the technique on pages 32–33 to add two 4mm black beads as eyes, then use a ¼ measure of white wool to reshape the back of the head and cover any black thread.

17 Next, make a thread using a ¹⁄₃₂ measure of white wool. Use the standard felting needle to attach it in the inside corner of the eye. Twist the thread to tighten it and use the fine felting needle to needle an eyelid along the top of the bead. Still using the fine felting needle, work the spare wool left over into the area above the eye to create a brow. Repeat on the other eye.

18 Card a ¾ measure of black wool and ¼ measure of white wool to make a charcoal grey mix. Use a few loose fibres to needle a tiny amount into the inner corners of the eyes and between the lids and the brow. Use the fine needle so as not to disturb the eyelids.

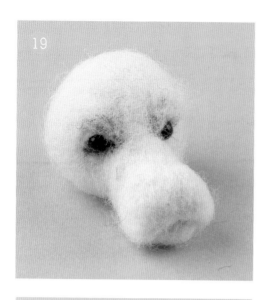

19 Still using the fine felting needle, lay a tiny web of white wool over the area and needle it to soften and blend the colour in. Trim with scissors, then needle a tiny dot of black merino wool into each eye corner to create more of an almond-shaped eye.

20 Divide a 1/32 measure of the charcoal grey mix in half. Use the fine felting needle to needle half of one piece into a triangle over the squared-off part of the muzzle, then needle the remaining part into a mouth line as shown with the standard felting needle.

21 Scratch the back of the polymer clay nose with the point of a needle to roughen it, then apply fast-acting white glue to the back and place it over the triangular area, facing forward and slightly down. While pushing on the nose, needle a 1/32 measure of white wool over the grey triangle above the polymer clay nose, using the fine felting needle. Use this to blend the visible grey triangle into the rest of the muzzle and build up the back of the nose. Put the detailed head to one side.

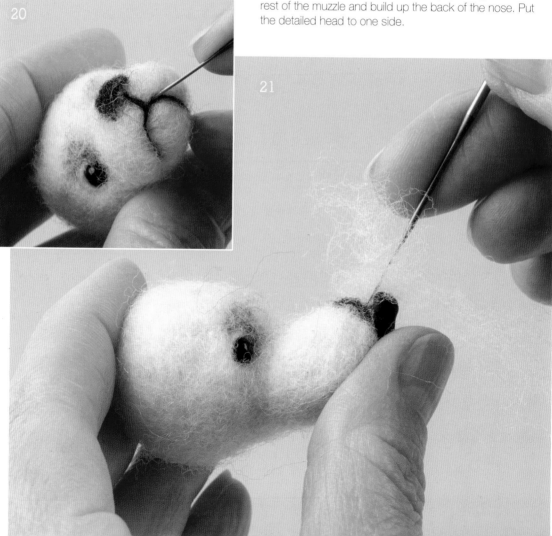

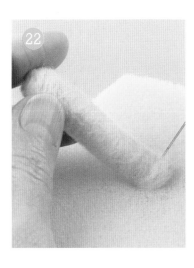
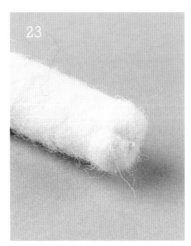
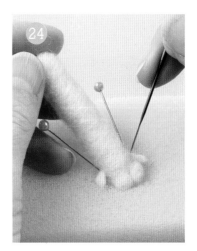

22 Build up the shape of a foot on the front part of one of the front legs using the fine felting needle and a 1/16 measure of white wool.

23 Use an embroidery needle and white thread to take a stitch from the centre of the bottom of the foot to the middle of the foot where it joins the leg.

24 Take two of the toes you made earlier and pin them in position on either side of the foot, then use the fine felting needle to implant them.

25 Using a tiny amount of the charcoal grey mix, needle a tiny amount of loose charcoal grey wool into the creases between the toes.

26 Still using the fine felting needle, squeeze and needle the foot from the sides to tighten it up. With tiny amounts of charcoal grey, add a large central pad to cover the stitch, then add four smaller pads around the centre as shown.

27 Add feet, toes, pads and details on the other legs in the same way.

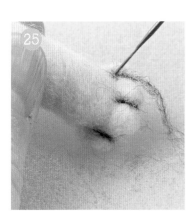
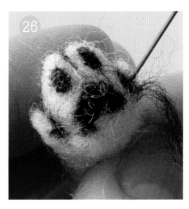
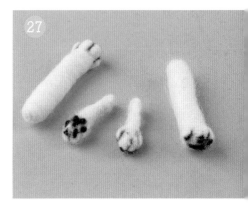

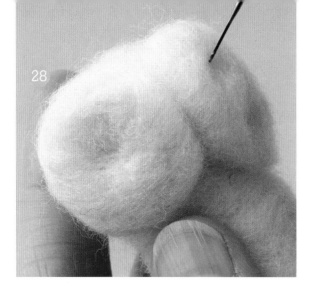

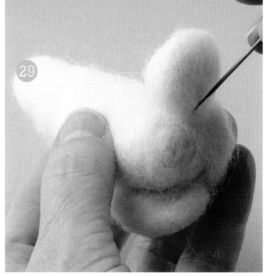

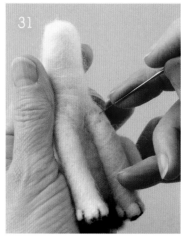

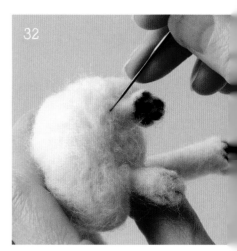

28 Take the three discs made in step 9. Implant two of the discs to the base of the body using the standard felting needle. Implant one on the back thoroughly all over, then implant one on the side just through the centre, leaving the edges loose.

29 Implant the third disc at the base of the body, implanting it just at the edge as shown.

30 Position the poodle's rear right leg between the centrally-attached side disc and the body and implant it using the standard felting needle; then position and implant the rear left leg on its side between the base-attached side disc and the body, as shown. Use some loose white wool to help implant, if necessary.

31 Implant the two front legs using the standard felting needle. To get the placement correct, place the feet flat on the ground and bring the body into position before felting them on.

32 Fill the gaps between the thighs and back discs to strengthen the area and build up the shaping of the rear legs and bottom. Use the fine felting needle and gradually add small amounts of loose wool.

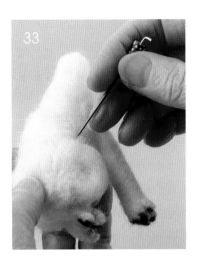

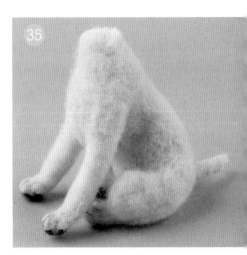

33 Continue to build up the shaping of the rear legs and bottom with the fine felting needle and loose wool. You will need approximately one whole measure, and another to fill the space over and between the thigh and back discs. Draw this wool up the back to create shaping and blend it in.

34 Continue shaping the additional wool around the lower part of the body, then implant the tail at the base as shown.

35 Build up the shaping of the upper body, using one measure across the back and shoulders (front legs) up to and around the neck; one measure across the chest and top of the front legs to help build up the musculature of the upper legs; and a ½ measure over the centre of the chest, drawing it in at the tummy line to create the distinctive chest shape.

36 Implant the head loosely with the standard felting needle.

37 Wrap a ½ measure of white wool around the neck and needle felt it in place. Change to the fine felting needle to shape the wool into the musculature of the neck.

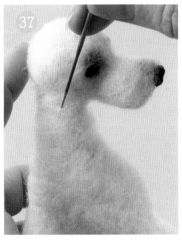

TIP

You might like to experiment with the head pointing in a different direction. Even such a seemingly small change can give your dog a lot of personality.

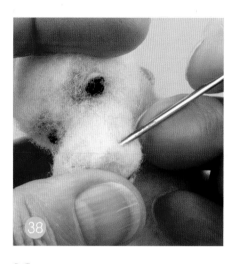

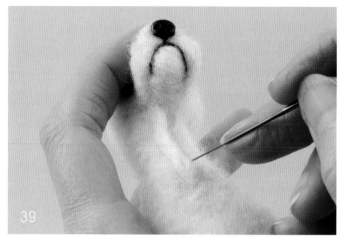

38 Use an embroidery needle to pull the jowls out a little.

39 Make a thread from a ¹⁄₃₂ measure of white wool. Lay it vertically on the neck, slightly off centre, and use a fine felting needle to attach it. Scratch out the ends until it blends smoothly into the bottom of the muzzle and the top of the chest. Add a second fold of skin in the same way on the other side of the neck.

40 Make a thread from a ¹⁄₁₆ measure of white wool and use the standard felting needle to securely attach it to the top of the head (see inset). Twist the other end until it starts coiling and buckling.

41 Lay the other end down nearby on the head. The thread will coil up into curls. Allow the curls to fill the immediate area.

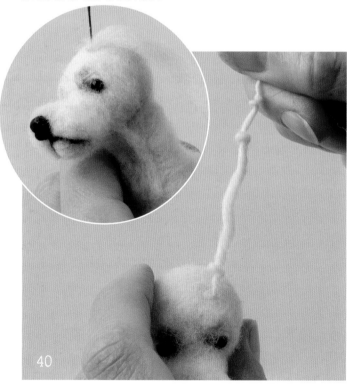

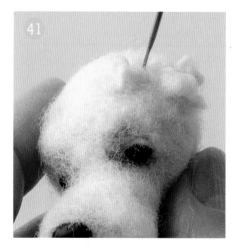

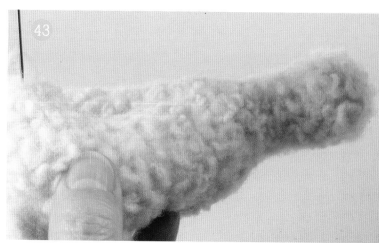

42 Continue to build up the curly coat over the head until the top is covered as shown.

43 Needle as many threads of wool as required to build up the curls over the neck, back, body and legs in the same way.

44 Add claws to each toe with the standard felting needle and a tiny touch of loose black wool. Once the wool is in, angle the scissors inwards and trim off the excess in a downward direction; this leaves it facing down like a real claw.

TIP

You can soften the effect by further needling the curls with the fine felting needle.

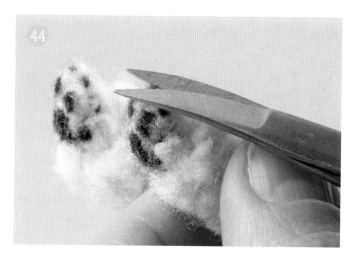

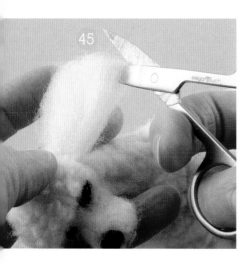

45 Implant the narrow end of the ear on the side of the head using the standard felting needle, then cut through the fold using the scissors.

46 Repeat on the other side. Tidy and trim the ears as necessary, and lightly tap the ends onto the body with the fine felting needle to help them hang realistically.

47 Pull and pile two half measures of white wool and use the standard needle to needle felt them to the end of the tail, one on the top and one on the bottom.

48 Loop the ends back into the tail and secure them using the standard needle.

49 Make another loop from an ⅛ measure of white wool and attach both ends to the end of the tail (see inset). Cut all of the loops with scissors.

50 Use scissors to trim the wool on the tail into a fluffy pompom, then make any other adjustments you feel necessary to finish.

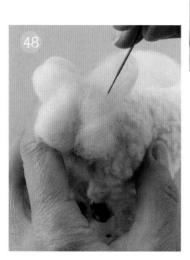

Sitting pretty

The happy boy on the right looks very different from the curly poodle in the project. You can achieve this look by using loose wool instead of threads of wool. Make sure you needle the wool enough to hold, but not so much that it becomes flattened. If you want to give him an open mouth, follow the instructions on page 110, then cover the sides of his muzzle with more loose wool. Give him a large top knot so that it all looks balanced and finish with a good trim.

Pug

This little pug's body is made using the same H-frame as the labrador retriever (see pages 50–57), but here the legs are outstretched in an appealing resting pose typical of the breed.

Using the correct technique it is possible to needle detailed pads on even the tiniest feet. The typical pug forehead is a challenge for even the most experienced needle felter, but with the aid of a reverse felting needle, softly wrinkled skin is more easily achievable.

Materials

Wool tops: 2½ measures of white Southdown; 2 measures of vanilla merino; 1 measure of black merino

Felting needles: 36T (standard); 38S (fine); 32S (reverse)

Two 4mm (¼in) black beads

Polymer clay nose (see page 36)

Embroidery needle

Fine beading needle

Strong black thread

Two 12cm (4¾in) lengths of chenille stick (pipe cleaner)

Wire cutters or strong scissors

Carding brushes

Pliers

Pen

Felting pad

Size

10cm (4in) long, 4.5cm (1¾in) high

Difficulty level

Expert

H-frame template

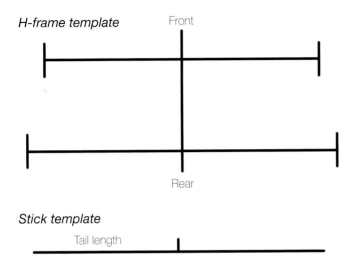

Front

Rear

TEMPLATES FOR THE PUG

All templates are shown at actual size. Dotted lines indicate the edge of shapes where loose wool (wavy lines) gradually becomes a part of the overall shape.

Stick template

Tail length

Basic body shape templates

These templates show the basic shapes of the body. Compare the pieces you make with these to ensure the sizes are correct.

Rear legs positioning (from above)

Ear

Front Back

Foot disc

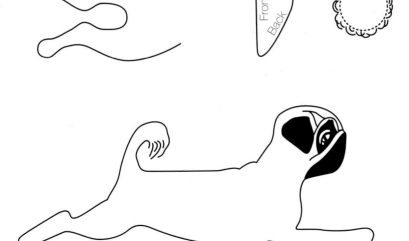

Reference for details

Nose

Eye

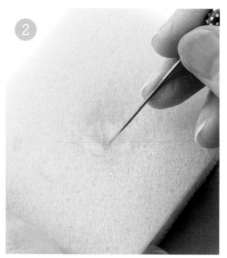

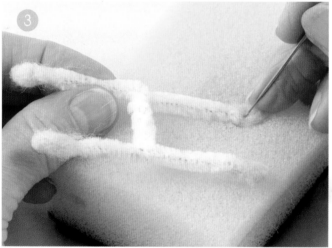

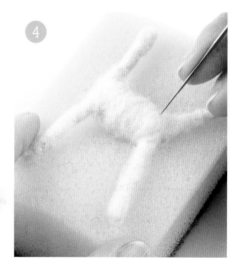

1 Use the carders to mix together (see pages 30–31) two measures of vanilla merino with two measures of white Southdown wool to make four whole measures of a light vanilla mix. This allows for a little extra.

2 Make an H-frame (see page 37) using the chenille sticks and the template on page 97, then needle felt a 1/16 measure of light vanilla wool into a disc using the fine felting needle. Keep the outside rough and fluffy, and the inside tighter.

3 Make four discs in total, and use the standard needle to felt a disc on to each foot of the H-frame, using the thicker centres as the base of the foot in each case.

4 Working one at a time, wrap an 1/8 measure of light vanilla wool around each leg and use the fine needle to needle felt it in place. Once all the legs are wrapped and felted, wrap and needle felt one complete measure of light vanilla wool around the body.

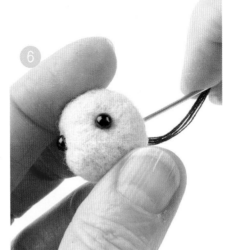

5 Use the standard felting needle to start to make a ball from one measure of light vanilla wool. Change to the fine felting needle once it holds together, and make sure it is very densely felted.

6 Following the instructions on pages 32–33, attach and secure a pair of 4mm beads to the ball as eyes. Because the head is so firm, you will likely not need to fill the back of the head as it will not distort. Cover the thread on the back of the head by scratching the wool around over it.

7 Use the standard felting needle to attach an ⅛ measure of charcoal mix (see page 30) to the front of the face as a muzzle. Use the fine felting needle to felt it onto the front of the head and shape it.

8 Pull and pile an ⅛ measure of charcoal mix wool into a 6cm (2⅜in) length. Twist the wool in the middle and attach the centre where the nose will be placed with the standard felting needle. It will look a little like a moustache.

9 Twist one end of the 'moustache' and draw it down the side of the muzzle so that it forms a bulge that runs down the side of the muzzle.

10 Holding the moustache bulge in place, use the fine felting needle to build the swell into one side of the upper jaw. Make sure that you stay within the line of the muzzle; do not take the wool over onto the rest of the head.

11 Repeat on the other side, felting into the crease from underneath to strengthen it.

12 Add dark patches around the eyes, using the fine felting needle and a 1/32 measure of the charcoal mix wool for each patch. Each patch should slant over the eye and join the muzzle, as shown.

13 Referring to the template for size, make two ears from the charcoal mix. You will need approximately a 1/16 measure of wool for each ear. Shape the front and back edges, and leave the other loose.

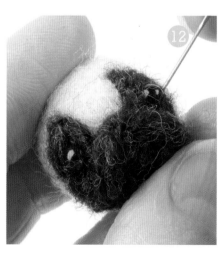

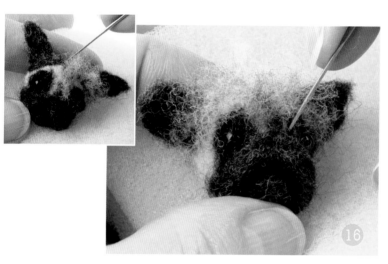

14 Use the standard felting needle to implant the loose edge onto the side of the head, then attach the second ear on the other side (see inset). The ears are not shaped yet; we are using them to help guide us for the shaping we are about to add.

15 Using a 1/32 measure of the charcoal wool mix and the fine felting needle, add a central stripe running upwards between the eyes from the muzzle. Needle this firmly and from the sides to form a solid, slightly ridged, shape. Using more 1/32 measures, add two more curved stripes running from near where the central stripe ends, round the ears, and down the sides of the face.

16 Use the reverse felting needle to work over the stripes to mix the wool and draw it out (see inset), then do the same around the edges of the eye patches.

17 Working stripe by stripe, fold the loose wool back over the head stripes and use the fine felting needle to work it back in. This draws the loose wool back into the head over the stripe, blending it in and reinforcing the ridge. This is the beginning of the distinctive wrinkles of the pug.

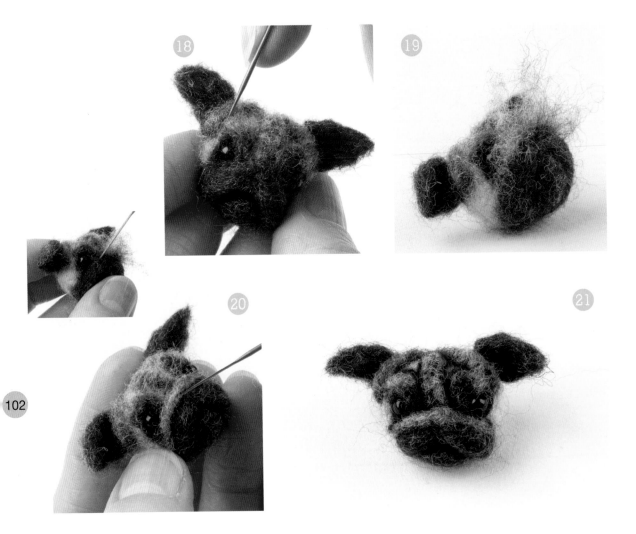

18 When you come to the eyes, fold the loose wool away from the edge of the black patch and felt it back in close to the original edge. This creates a small wrinkle around each eye.

19 Begin to produce a crease that runs right along where the muzzle meets the rest of the head. Pull out a stripe that runs all the way from the points where the furthest parts of the eyepatches meet the muzzle on either side.

20 Work deep with the standard reverse felting needle to draw out light fur from the area (see inset), then use the fine felting needle to loop the drawn-out fur back in, creating a white ridge across the muzzle. Work it back in from all directions to create the distinctive shape.

21 Use small amounts of loose black wool to add fine stripes that run alongside the main stripes, highlighting them and further emphasising the wrinkles. Needle the fibres in with the fine felting needle. You will need approximately a $1/32$ measure of black wool in total.

22 The black stripes surround two triangular areas on the head. Add a tiny spot of black in these using a little loose black wool and the fine felting needle (see inset). Felt these in deeply. Next, use the standard reverse felting needle and draw out the colours from deep within the ball to make these triangles stand out more.

23 Using the fine felting needle and tiny loose touches of the light vanilla wool mix, add highlights across the lighter areas of the head and face. Less is more. Keep these highlights on the highest parts of the ridges, not down in the wrinkles.

24 Add a pure white flash above where the nose will sit using the fine felting needle and a tiny touch of pure white Southdown wool; then add two small dots of pure black merino wool in the upper inner corners of each eye patch as shown.

25 Make a thread from a tiny amount of black merino and felt it into place as the mouth using the fine felting needle. Work the wool into and under the mouth crease you made in steps 10 and 11. Accentuate the line by repeatedly jabbing the needle in along the bottom of the line.

26 Shape the ears by working the standard felting needle deep into the point where it joins the head. The ears will gradually curl over into a cupped shape. Use the fine felting needle to work any loose wool that emerges back into the ear. Put the head to one side for the moment.

103

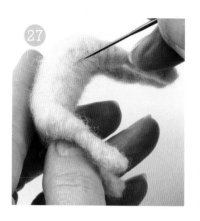

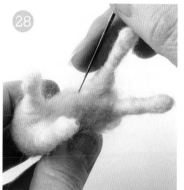

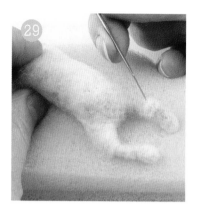

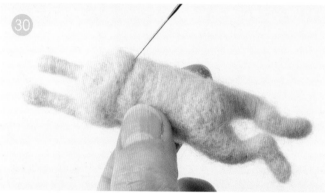

27 Take the H-frame and bend the front and back legs down. Using the fine needle, add a ¼ measure of the light vanilla wool mix to the bottom to add shaping to the body. With this shaping in place, add an ⅛ measure to the shoulders (front legs) and thighs (tops of the rear legs). Use the template as reference for shaping.

28 Still using the fine needle continue developing the shaping, adding a ¼ measure of the light vanilla wool mix to the chest, another across the back and another to the underside.

29 Bend the front legs out straight forwards, and the back legs out at an angle as shown. Wrap a ¹⁄₃₂ measure of the light vanilla wool mix around the bend in one of the rear legs and use the fine felting needle to develop the shaping around the joint.

30 Use a ¹⁄₃₂ measure of the light vanilla wool mix to develop the joint on the other back leg in the same way, then add the fat shaping. Using the light vanilla mix and the fine felting needle throughout, needle felt a ¹⁄₁₆ measure onto either flank around his tummy, then pull and pile a ¹⁄₁₆ measure into a 5cm (2in) length and lay it across his back from shoulder to shoulder as a little roll of fat. Needle felt this in place to form a ridge, then felt another behind it in exactly the same way. Use the felting needle to accentuate the fold between the ridges.

TIP

If any gaps appear while bending the legs, add webs of light vanilla wool mix and felt in to cover them, using the fine felting needle.

31 Use the standard felting needle to implant an ⅛ measure of the light vanilla wool mix into the neck area, leaving plenty of loose wool free. Pull some loose strands out of the back of the pug's head.

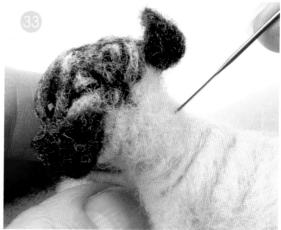

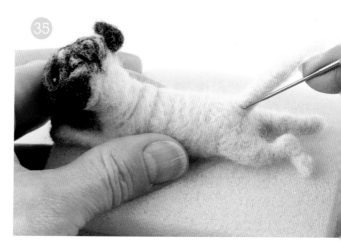

32 Using the standard felting needle and the loose wool from both sides, implant the head securely onto the body.

33 Wrap a ¼ measure of light vanilla wool mix round the join between the head and the neck, then use a fine felting needle to felt a chubby neck. Felt in another ⅛ measure on the back of the head and down the neck.

34 Use the stick technique to make a 4cm (1½in) tail using a cocktail stick, a ¼ measure of the light vanilla wool mix and the fine felting needle. Use the standard felting needle to gently tease out the end.

35 Implant the tail using the standard felting needle.

36 Curl the tail over and use the fine felting needle to lightly tap the loose wool at the end of it back into the base of the tail. This will lightly hold it in a curled position.

37 Use the fine felting needle to add a 1/16 measure of the light vanilla mix around each of the rear feet to bulk them up a little, then add some detail on the base of each of the feet as shown; one larger central bean-shaped pad, and four surrounding smaller round pads. Use the fine felting needle to needle small amounts of charcoal mix into place before cutting them off flush with the foot. It is the ends of the charcoal wool that appear as toe pads.

38 Use the standard felting needle to make a hole in the muzzle for the polymer clay nose nose to fit into, just below the white ridge.

39 To finish, scratch the back of the nose with the point of a needle to roughen it, then apply fast-acting white glue to the back and place it over the hole.

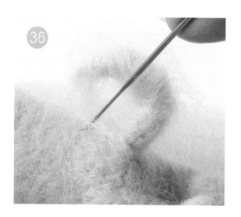

Appealing pugs

You can choose dark- or light-coloured wrinkles. If you choose to have very light-coloured wrinkles, as in the pug on the right-hand side here, use the same vanilla mix as on the body. Pure white is only suitable for small highlights. Carefully work along the ridges with thin webs of wool. If they get flattened, lift them by inserting an embroidery needle. If you want sharp definition, add more black to the furrows.

Going further

When you have finished, you may have a little dog that you are proud of just as it is. However, you may want to go on and finish it to perfection and add extra details to make it look even more lifelike. Sometimes adjustments can improve the look of a dog. Be adventurous, try new ways. There is no right and wrong way to create a little creature from fluff.

Designing your own dog

If you have worked through the projects, you have all the skills you need to go on to make your own breed of needle felted dog! Using the techniques you have learnt in this book, you can go on to make other dog breeds, like the West Highland terriers below.

I can design dogs and make the templates, and even tell you roughly how much wool to use but as no two felted animals are exactly alike, there can be no definitive pattern for finishing off. It helps to have pictures of the breed to which you can refer. Do not be afraid to make changes at the end that will enhance the look of your dog.

TIPS FOR MAKING YOUR OWN DOGS

- Study the dog you wish to make and take photographs from all angles for reference. A photograph that is the actual size of the dog you are making is good for keeping a check on the proportions. You could also make a few simple sketches.

- Think about the construction from the inside out. A dog with thin legs will always require a wire armature for stability, for example. The pose of the dog may also have an influence on your choice of construction.

- Pay special attention to the detail. If markings on the coat need to be very precise, map them out roughly first with tiny tacking stitches or marker pen dots.

- For dogs with a long coat, ensure your underlying structure is a good shape and nice and firm structure, then implant the coat from the bottom upwards so that the roots are covered over.

West Highland terriers
These are made like the cocker spaniel (see pages 40–49) but with a stockier body, shorter muzzle, tail and legs. Looped threads of wool are scissored into a chrysanthemum-shaped head allowing the eyes, nose and perky little triangular shaped ears to peep through. The tail is thicker at the base, trimmed to a carrot shape.

Dogs in different sizes

Some people like working on a larger scale, but a dog like this life-sized Chihuahua takes many hours to complete. To cut down on needle-felting time, you can buy soft, partially felted material called pre-felt. Cut it into strips and wrap it firmly around all the armature wires. Bind it with wool yarn so that it stays in place, then continue to needle felt as normal.

Adjusting the templates

If you want to make a larger or smaller version of the dogs in the projects, you can alter the size of the template. However, remember that your sculpture is three-dimensional and so the number of measures required to cover an armature doubled in size will be significantly more than doubled.

Similarly, if you wish to reduce the scale, the amount of wool required to cover the armature will be much less.

Working from templates alone without measures should not be a problem now that you have worked your way through all the projects. You will be familiar with roughly how much wool to use, so work freely and put your experience to the test.

Detailing your dogs

After you have completed the projects or a dog of your own, you might like to add some extra details for character and realism.

Eyelashes

Eyelashes are great subtle details for adding realism to your dog.

1 Implant tiny amounts of suitably coloured wool all along the inside of the top eyelid.

2 Dip an embroidery needle into thin white glue. Wipe the loaded needle carefully over and under the lashes so they are lightly coated in glue. Gently dab off any excess glue.

3 Arrange and separate lashes with an embroidery needle and trim with a small pair of scissors.

TIP

Use a shield of thin card to protect handmade eyes from glue or use glass eyes.

Claws

Larger needle-felted dogs look more convincing with realistic claws. This is an easy way to make nicely shaped claws which are delicate enough to enhance the dog's toes. Just a hint of a claw or none at all is fine on a tiny dog; their scale allows simplicity.

1 Implant a tiny amount of silk fibre into the end of a toe.

2 Dip an embroidery needle into thin white glue. Wipe the loaded needle over and under the silk, then dab off any excess glue.

3 Before the glue dries, pinch the silk fibres together. Trim with the scissors pointing downwards.

4 Once trimmed, hold over a cocktail stick to create a softly curled claw. Trim again if necessary.

Open mouth

After spending hours needle felting a dog's head, it takes courage to get the scissors and cut open the muzzle! Needle felting is a voyage of discovery and it is worth trying new ways.

1 Take a firmly felted dog's head and needle felt a mouth line. This is so you know accurately where to cut.

2 Hold your breath while you cut along the mouth line with sharp scissors!

3 Pull open the mouth and reshape the muzzle as necessary. Add extra detail to the mouth if you choose.

4 Implant a little tongue that peeps out of the slightly open mouth.

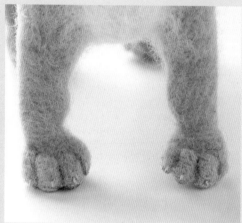

Accessories

Tiara

The tiara is made from looped wire. To get nice round loops, I used a jeweller's peg board.

1 Leaving approximately 2cm (¾in) of straight wire at the end, loop the wire around the jeweller's peg board to form a decorative pattern.

2 Trim the wire 3cm (1¼in) from the other end, then bend over the tips of both ends with pliers.

3 Mould the piece around a cylindrical object to form a rounded tiara shape.

4 Glue or wire on pearls or sparkly beads to decorate.

Hats and bands

Wool felt (i.e. ready-made felt) soaked in diluted white glue and left to dry will hold the shape of any object you mould it around. Using this method you can make hats in all shapes and sizes, as shown on the right. These can be decorated as you like; with ribbon, feathers or beads.

The headband (left) is simply a length of wire cut and shaped to fit the dog's head. After threading on tiny beads, turn the ends over. A flower was attached to this example with fine wire.

Index